CAT SAYINGS

wit & wisdom
from the whiskered ones

By Bradford G. Wheler

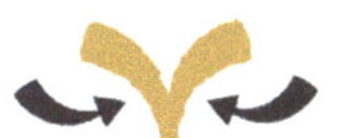

BookCollaborative.com
Cazenovia, NY 13035

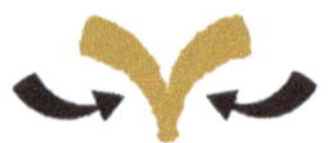

BookCollaborative.com
PO box 403
Cazenovia, NY 13035
BookCollaborative.com@gmail.com

ISBN-13 978-0-9822538-4-7

Library of Congress Control Number: 2012910062
Quotations, Cats, Art, Humor & Wit

PRINTER IN THE UNITED STATES OF AMERICA

Cover design by AuthorSupport.com
Interior design by Adina Cucicov, Flamingo Designs

Table of Contents

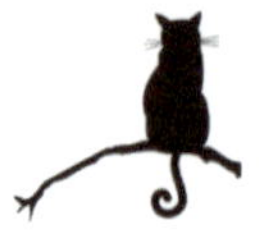

Introduction

I would like to thank everyone who participated in this project. In particular, I wanted to thank the artists and photographers who contributed their original works to this book.

It was exciting to check my email and find a wonderful range of new submissions from a wide variety of artists and photographers. The book features 60 artists form 9 different countries. Many of the artists in this book are full time professional artists or photographers. Others love painting and photographing as a hobby. They exhibit a wonderful range of artistic styles. All are cat lovers.

I was very pleased to see how many of these artists are currently involved in animal rescue projects, giving generously of both their time and talent.

I established BookCollaborative.com to publish books based on the content provided by artists. The goal is to create a collaborative community to promote art in general. At the same time, artists have the opportunity to promote their own artwork in books. I also want it to be interesting and fun. For more information go to www.BookCollaborative.com.

In selecting images for CAT SAYINGS, I tried to be inclusive. However, some artwork simply didn't fit the theme of this book. Other artwork did not make the cut due to vari-

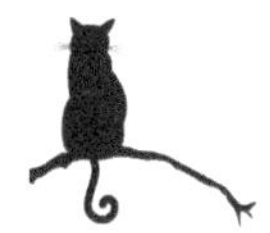

ous factors, such as missing the deadline, low image resolution, etc.

Printing color books with Lightening Source Inc's on demand system is about six times as expensive as printing black and white books. This factor limits the page count of a reasonably priced color book. It my hope that as technology progresses, the price for color on demand printing will come down. This would allow greater flexibility in the size of color books as well as the number of pages.

This book would not have been possibly without the help of many others. They include Adina Cucicov of Flamingo Design, who has done a beautiful job with the book's interior design, Nancy Kelner who turns my sloppy first drafts into a workable format, Brian Hoke of Bentley Hoke Consulting who helped with all things web related, and Simon, Ethan, and others from the Apple store One to One training team who patiently keep teaching me. I would like to thank my lovely wife Julie for her support on this project and everything else.

I'm sure this book includes errors. For those I apologize.

Most of all I hope people enjoy *"CAT SAYINGS; wit and wisdom from the whiskered ones."*

Bradford G. Wheler
Cazenovia, NY
September 2012

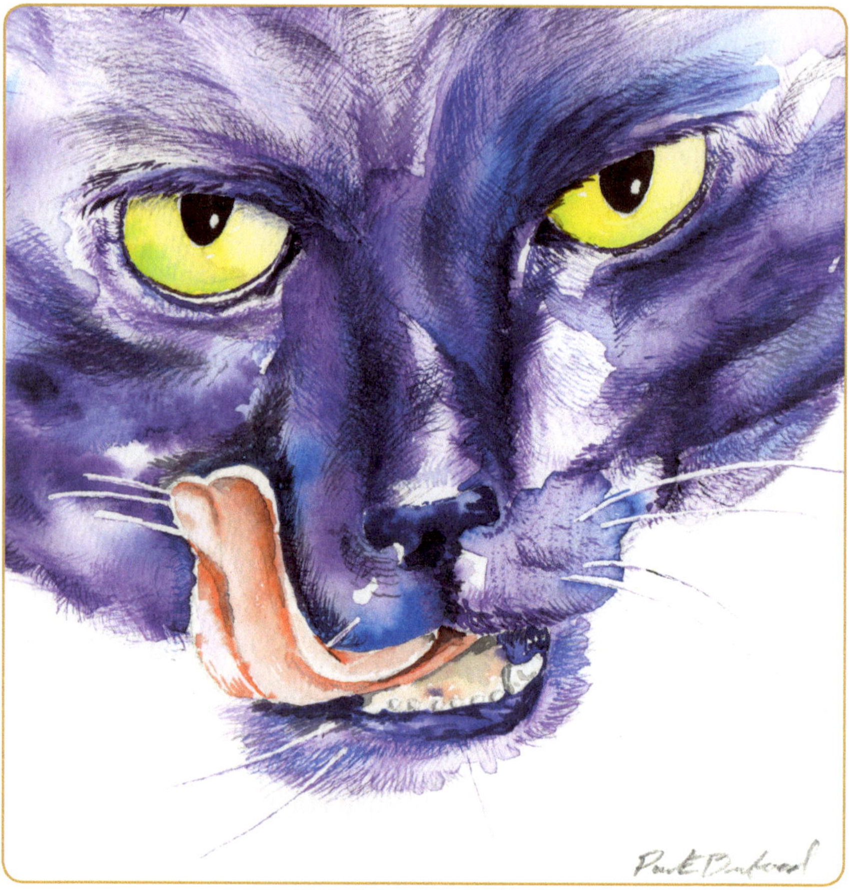

Paul Buford

CHAPTER 1

Cats Rule

There are no ordinary cats.
Colette, (1873–1954)

To a cat, human beings are an inferior, servile race, always to be kept in their places, with occasional rewards if they perform well.
Haskel Frankel, (1926–1999)

The real objection to the great majority of cats is their insufferable air of superiority.
P.G.Wodehouse, (1881–1975)

Every cat is really the most beautiful woman in the room.
Edward Verral Lucas, (1868–1938)

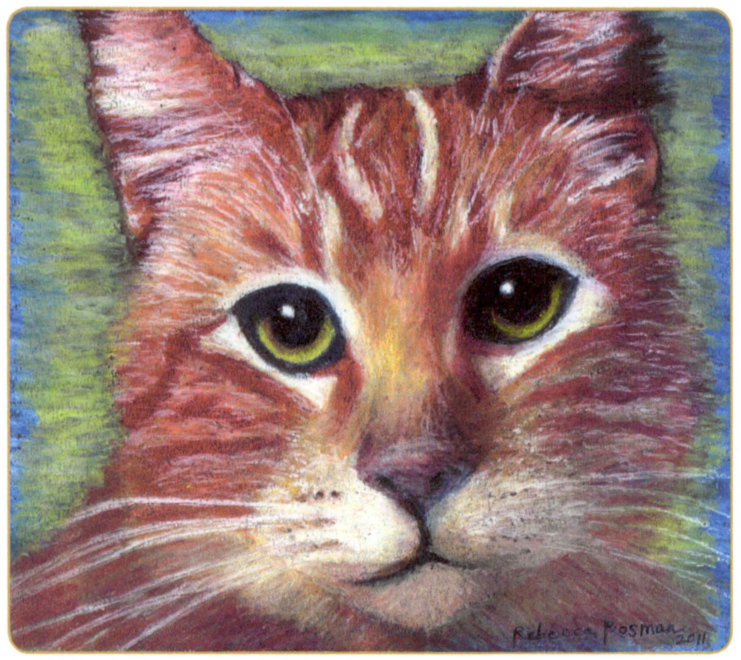

Rebecca Rosman

Of all God's creatures there is only one that cannot be made the slave of the lash. That one is the cat. If man could be crossed with the cat, it would improve man, but it would deteriorate the cat.

Mark Twain, (1835–1910)

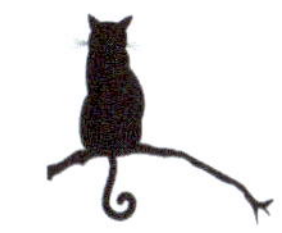

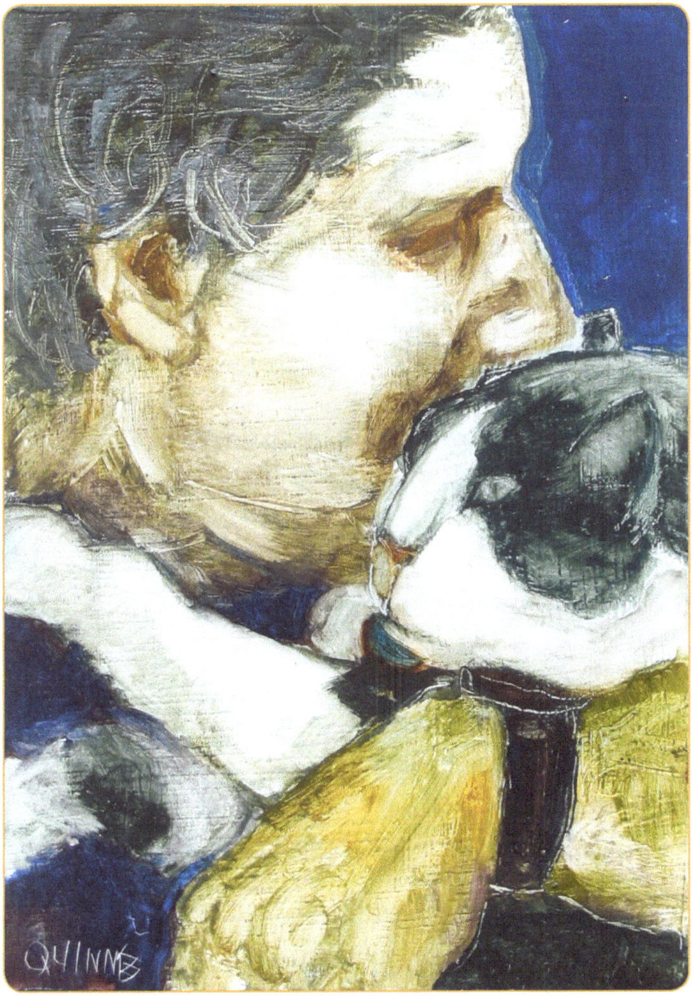

Quinne Fokes

You are my cat and I am your human.

Hilaire Belloc, (1870–1953)

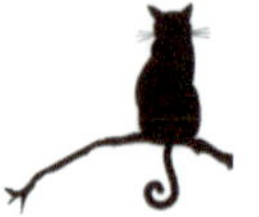

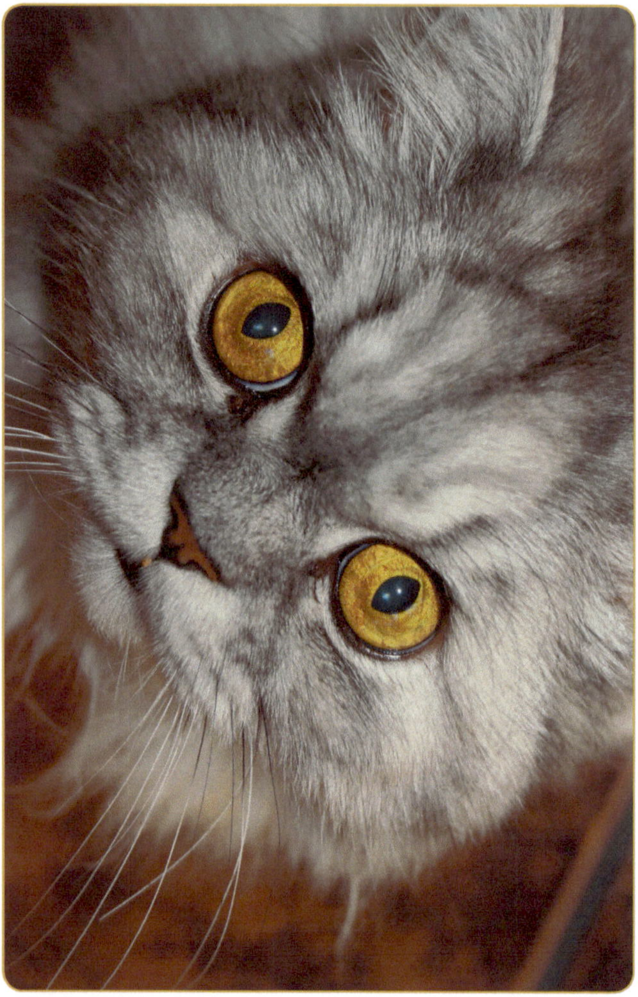

Karen Commings

A cat is nobody's fool.

Heywood Broun, (1888–1939)

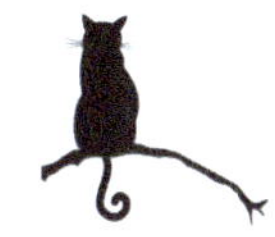

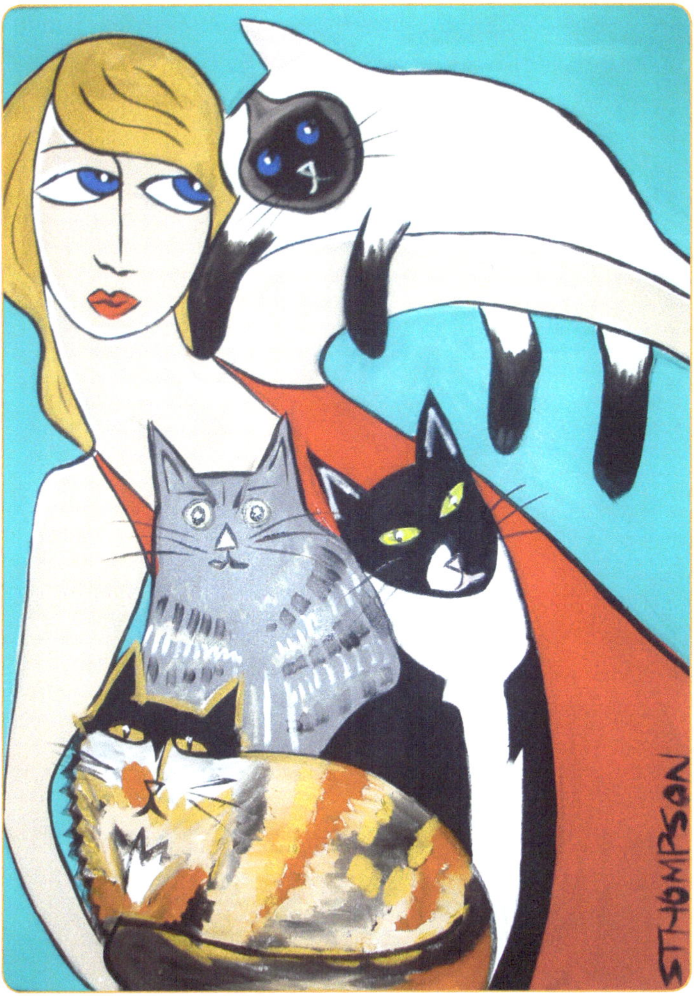

Samantha Thompson

One cat just leads to another.

Ernest Hemingway, (1899–1963)

Cats are intended to teach us that not everything in nature has a function.

Garrison Keillor, (b. 1942)

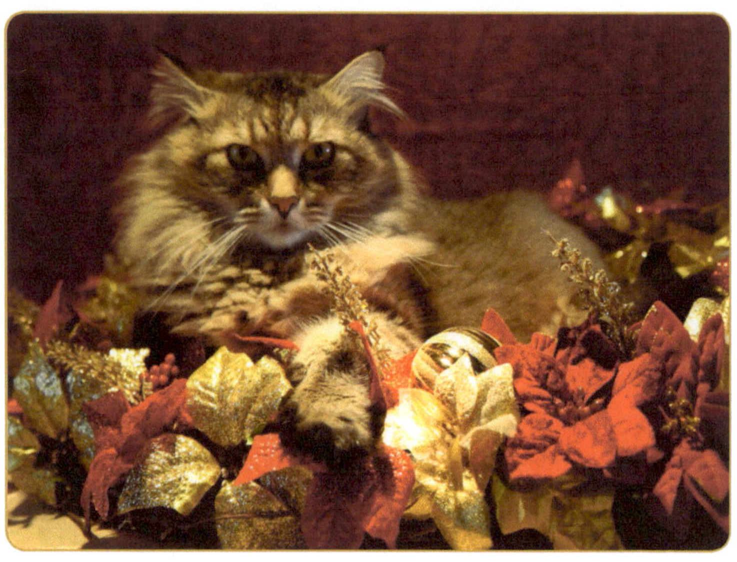

Sue Spina

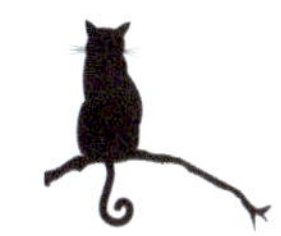

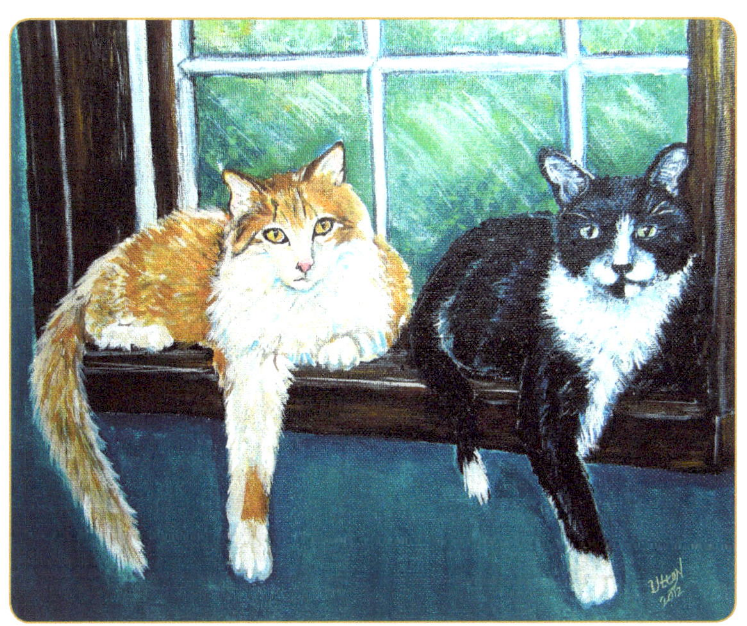

Pamela Utton

The cats knew what was what.
They were the boss. I was the pet.

Neil Chesanow, (b. 1944)

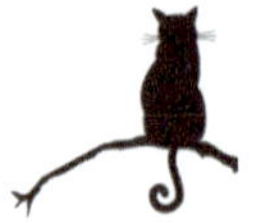

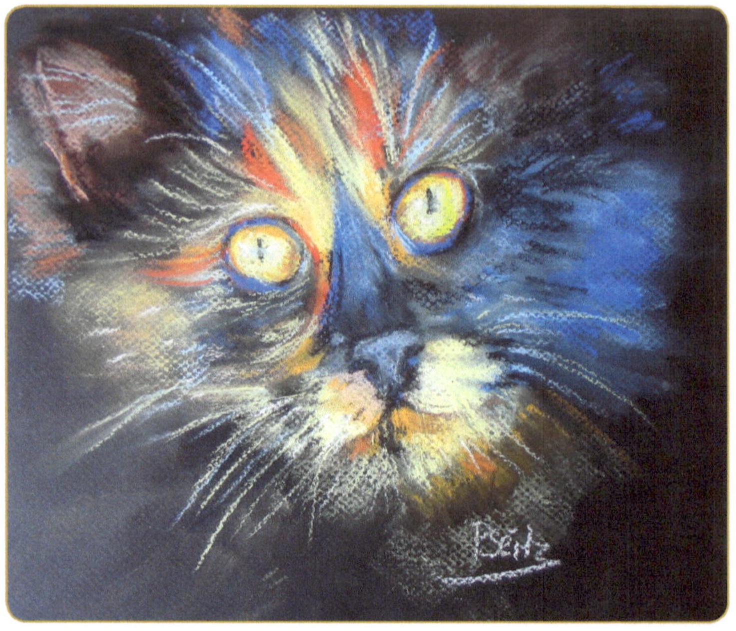

Patricia Elliot Seitz

Those who play with cats must expect to be scratched.
Miguel De Cervantes, (1547–1616)

A man who carries a cat by the tail learns something he can learn in no other way.
Mark Twain, (1835–1910)

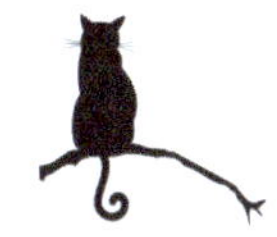

Some men are born to cats, others have cats thrust upon them.

Gilbert Millstein, (1916–1999)

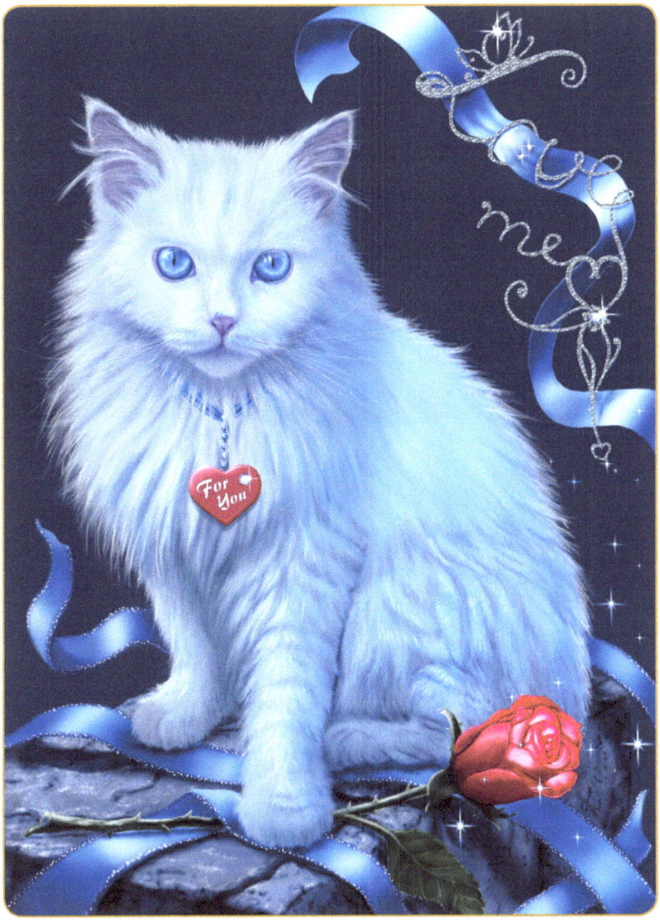

Tatjana Willms

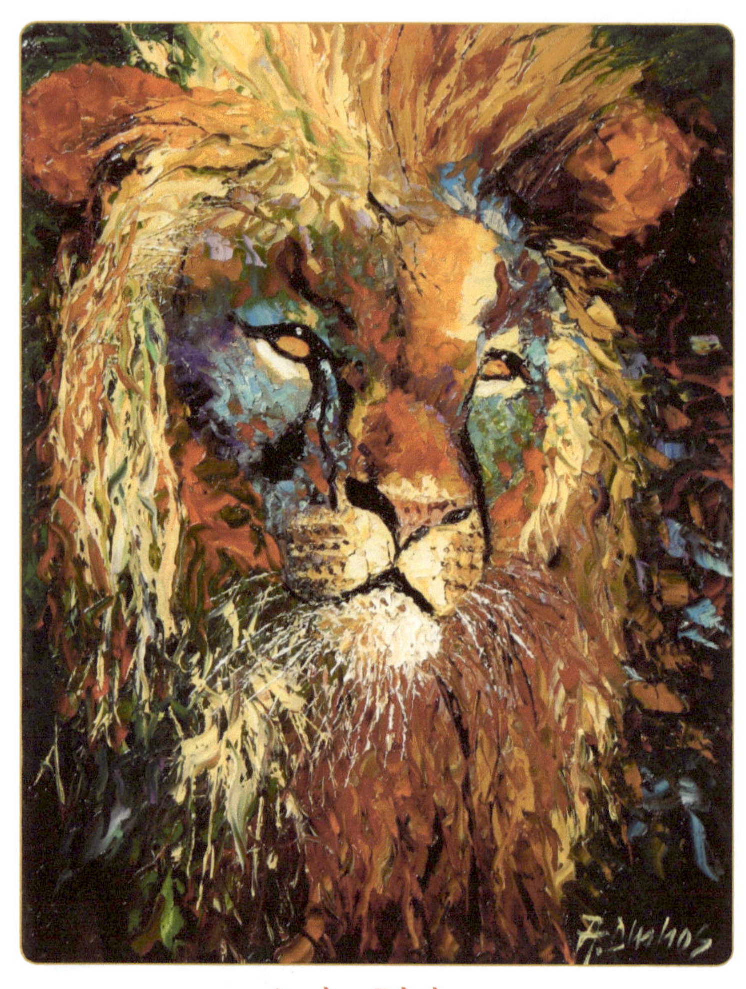

Andre Dluhos

CHAPTER 2

Wild Cats

An optimist is someone who gets treed by a lion but enjoys the scenery.

Walter Winchell, (1897–1972)

A lion's work hours are only when he's hungry; once he's satisfied, the predator and prey live peacefully together.

Chuck Jones, (1912–2002)

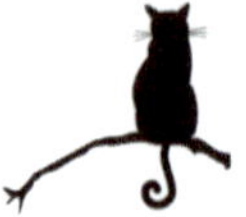

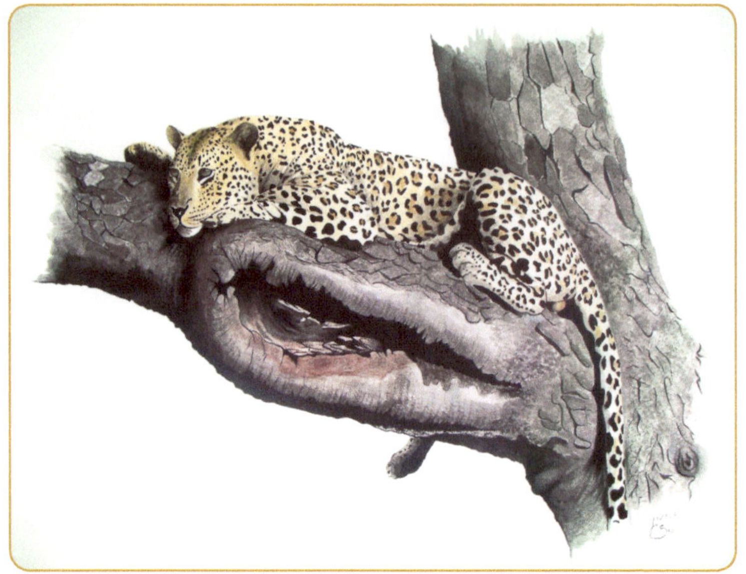

Angela Skea

A leopard does not change his spots,
or change his feeling that spots
are rather a credit.
Ivy Compton-Burnett, (1884–1969)

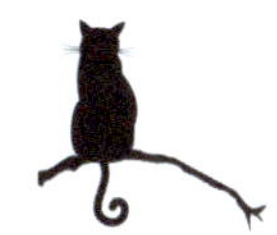

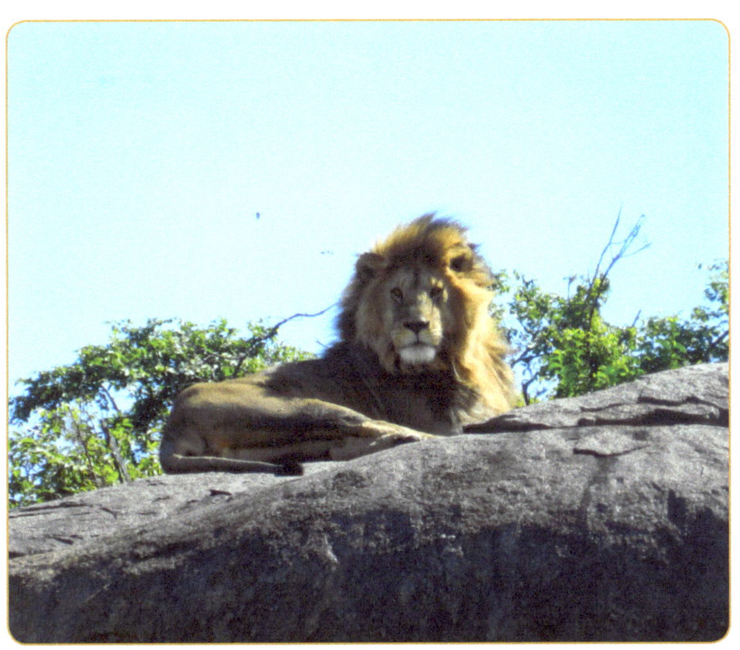

Garrett Redmond

At a certain point,
even if the one alpha male is dominant,
at a certain point there's a younger lion that
is stronger, and everyone knows it.

Josh Lucas, (b. 1971)

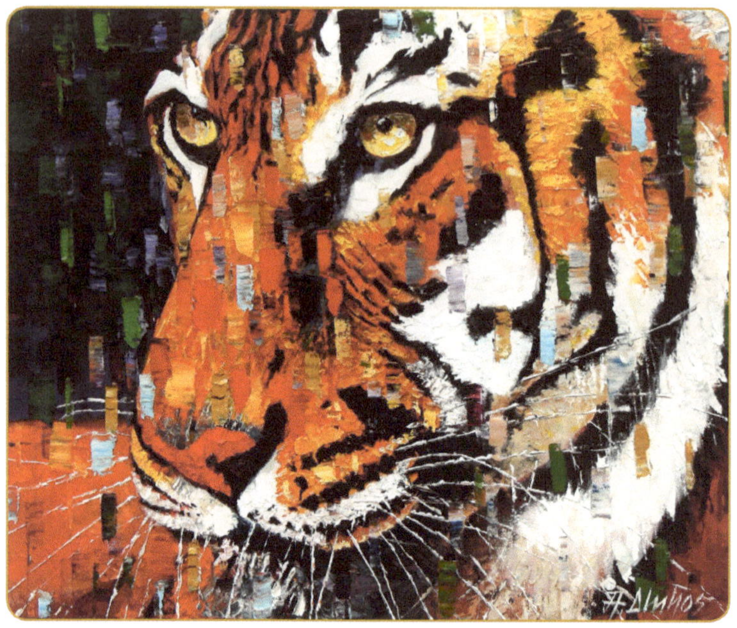

Andre Dluhos

An infallible method of conciliating a tiger is to allow oneself to be devoured.

Konrad Adenauer, (1876–1967)

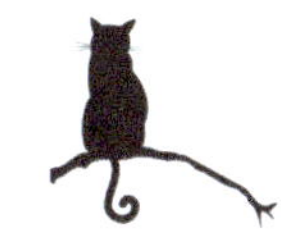

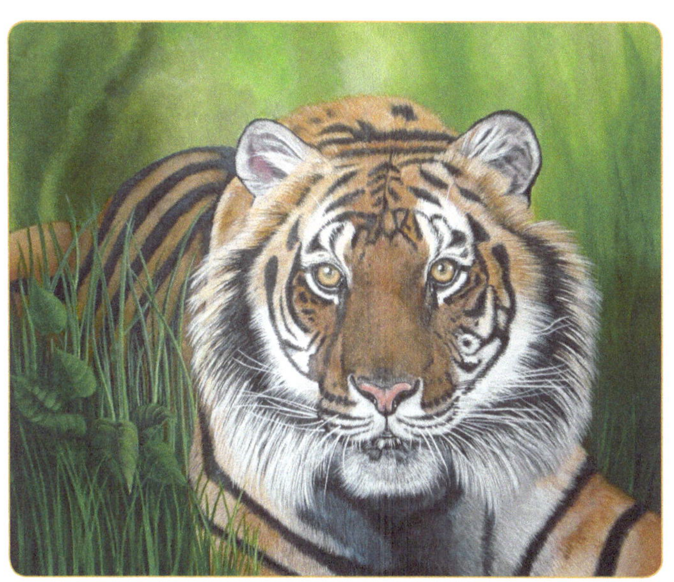

Jennifer Deakin

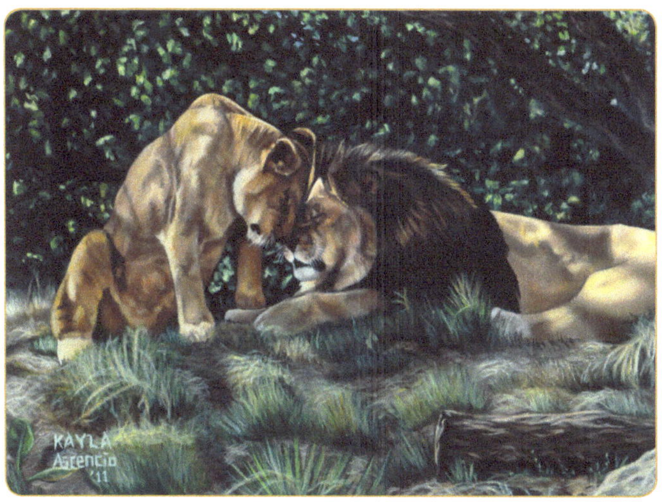

Kayla Ascencio

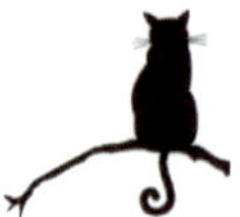

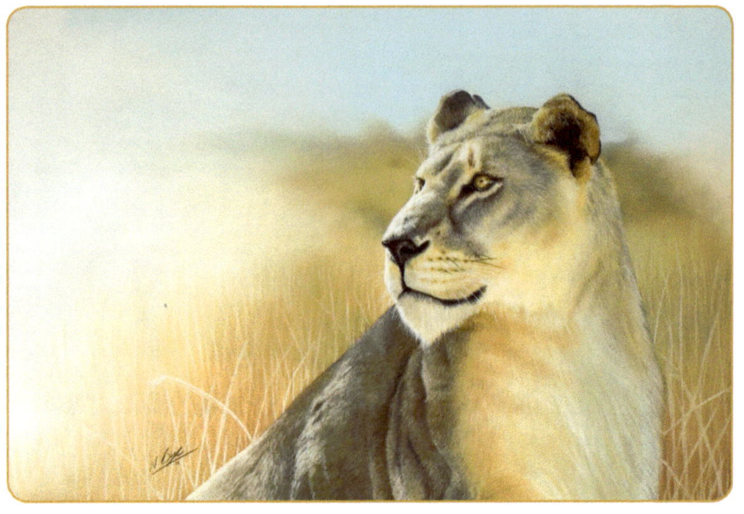

Nathan Bye

Courage is poorly housed that dwells in numbers; the lion never counts the herd that are about him, nor weighs how many flocks he has to scatter.
Aaron Hill, (1685–1750)

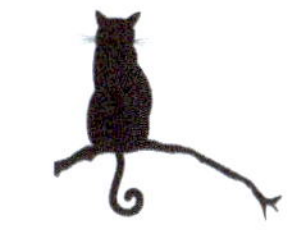

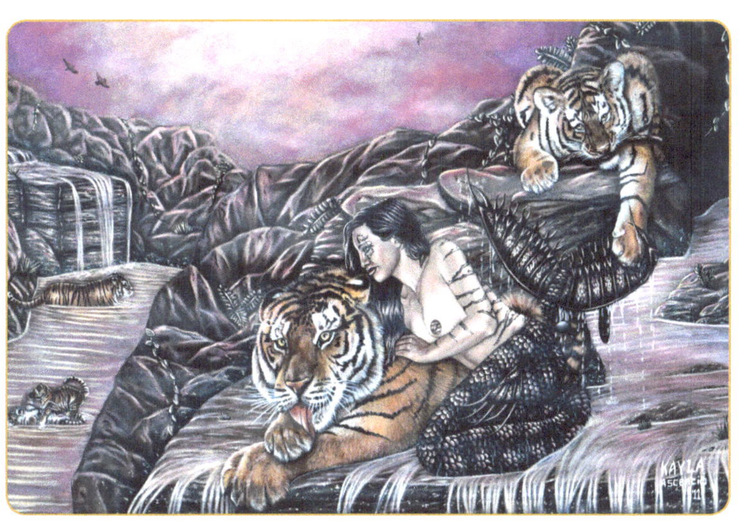

Kayla Ascencio

Every woman should have four pets in her life. A mink in her closet, a jaguar in her garage, a tiger in her bed, and a jackass who pays for everything.

Paris Hilton, (b. 1981)

I am not afraid of an army of lions led by a sheep; I am afraid of an army of sheep led by a lion.

Alexander the Great, (356–323 BC)

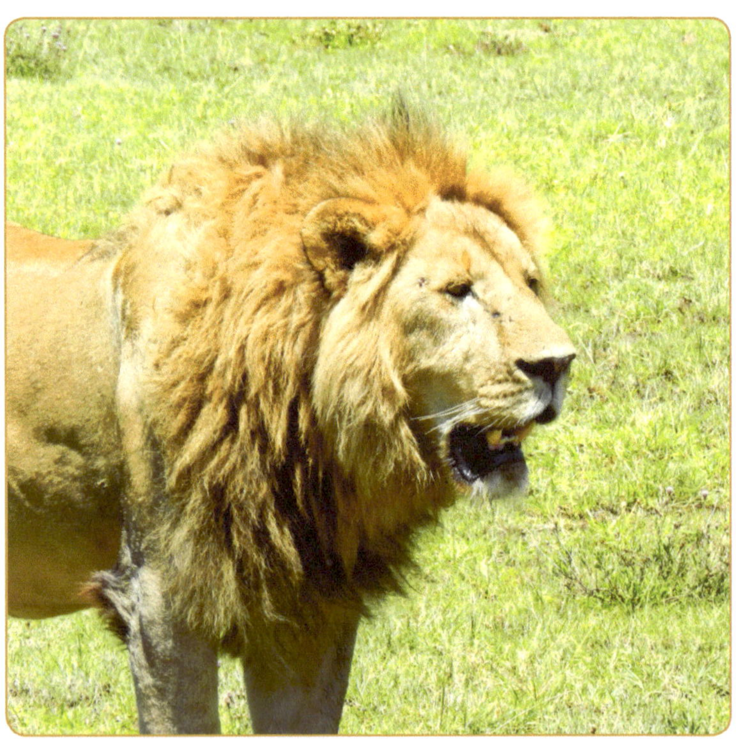

Garrett Redmond

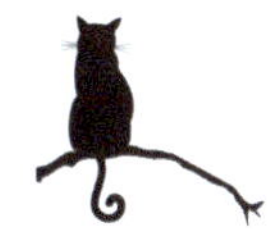

CHAPTER 2
Wild Cats

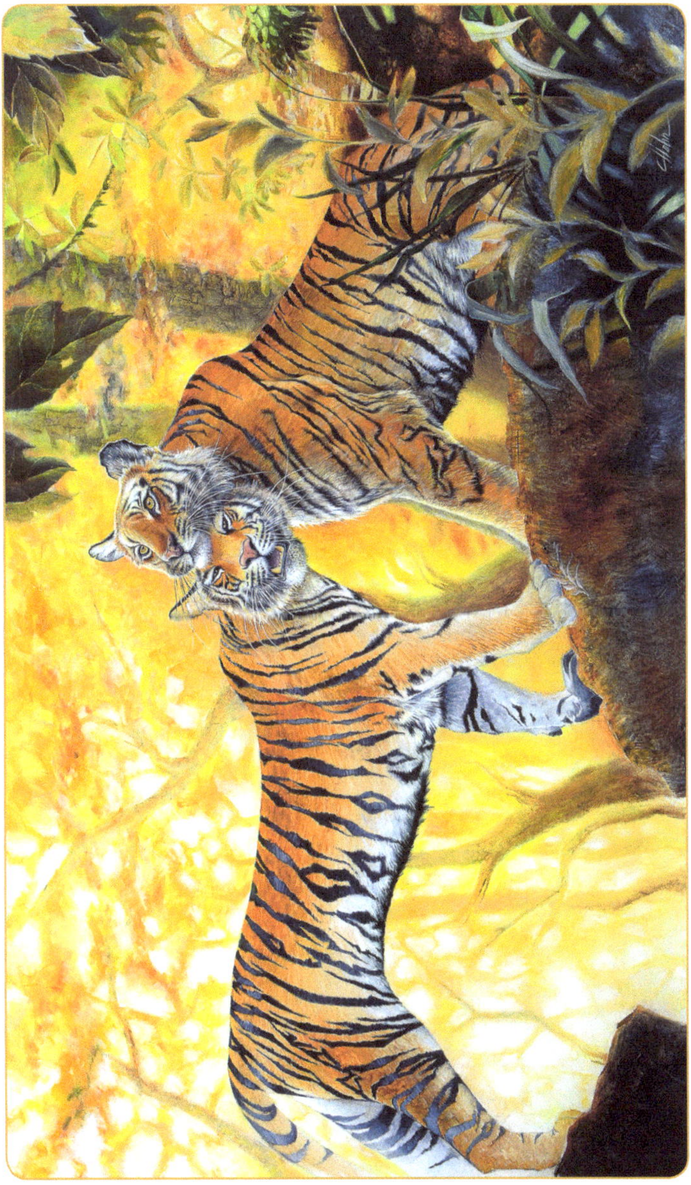

Claudia Hahn

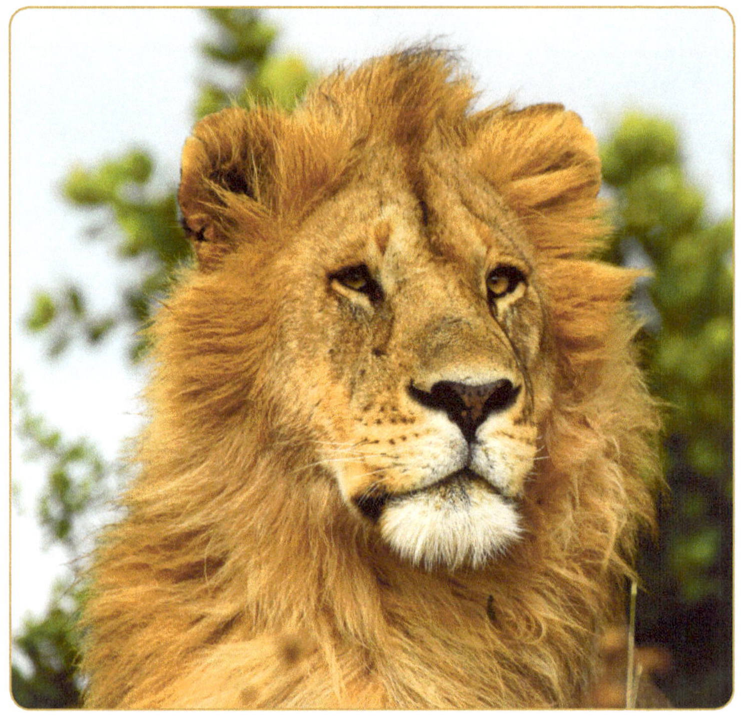

Roland Anderson

I never thought much of the courage of a lion tamer. Inside the cage he is at least safe from people.

George Bernard Shaw, (1856–1950)

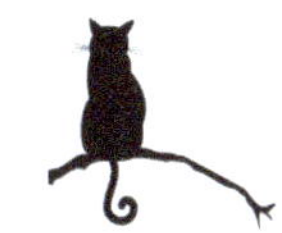

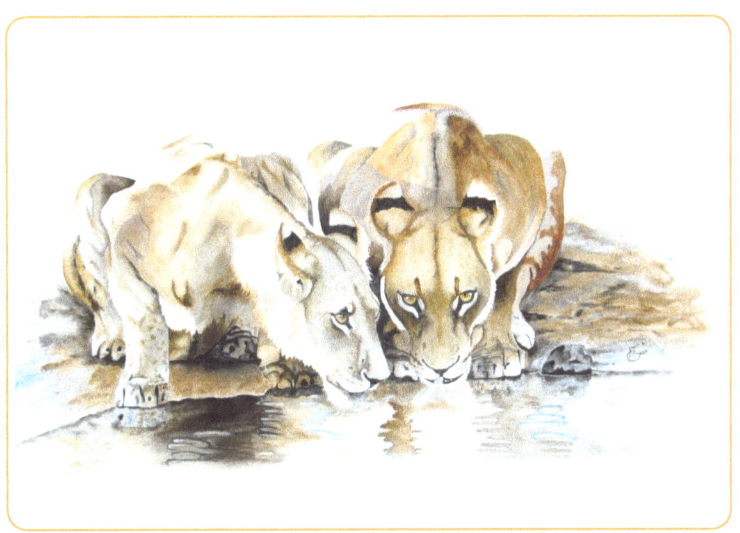

Angela Skea

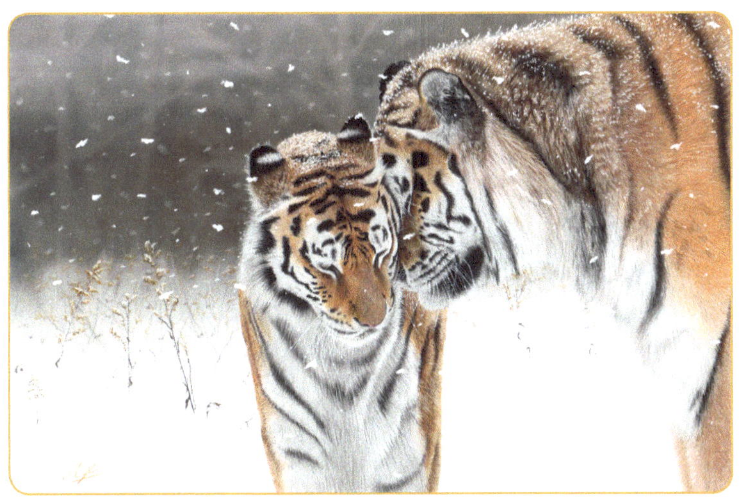

Nathan Bye

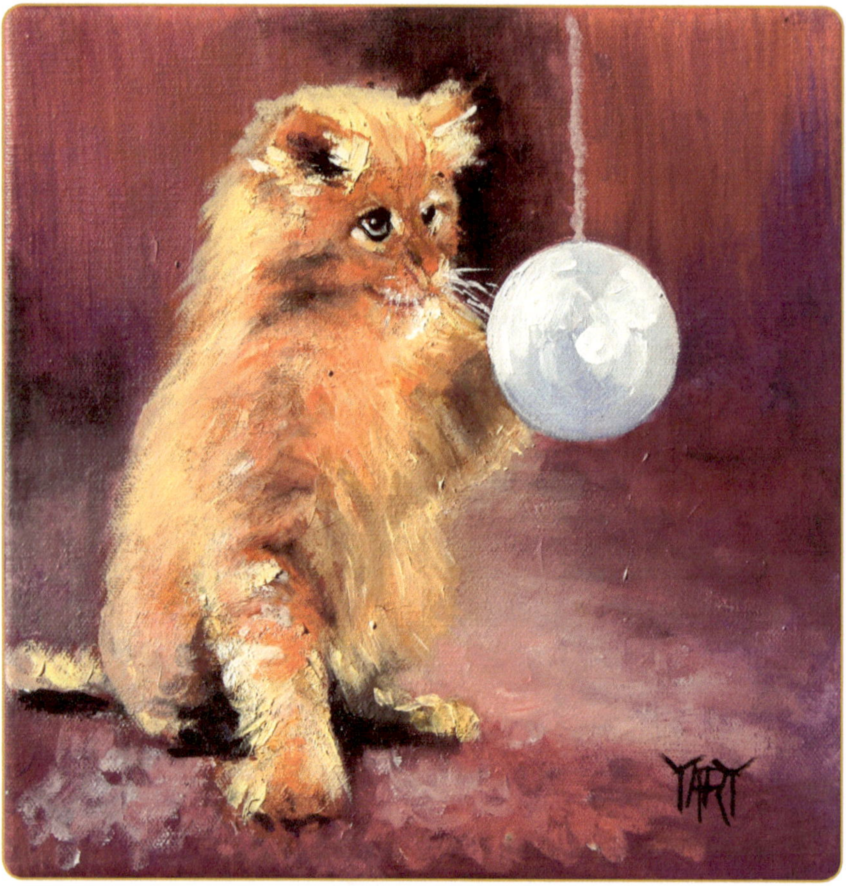

Andre Dluhos

CHAPTER 3

Kittens

A kitten is the rosebud in the garden of the animal kingdom.

Robert Southey, (1774–1843)

An ordinary kitten will ask more questions than any five-year-old boy.

Carl Van Vechten, (1880–1964)

No matter how much cats fight, there always seem to be plenty of kittens.

Abraham Lincoln, (1809–1865)

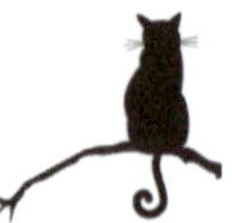

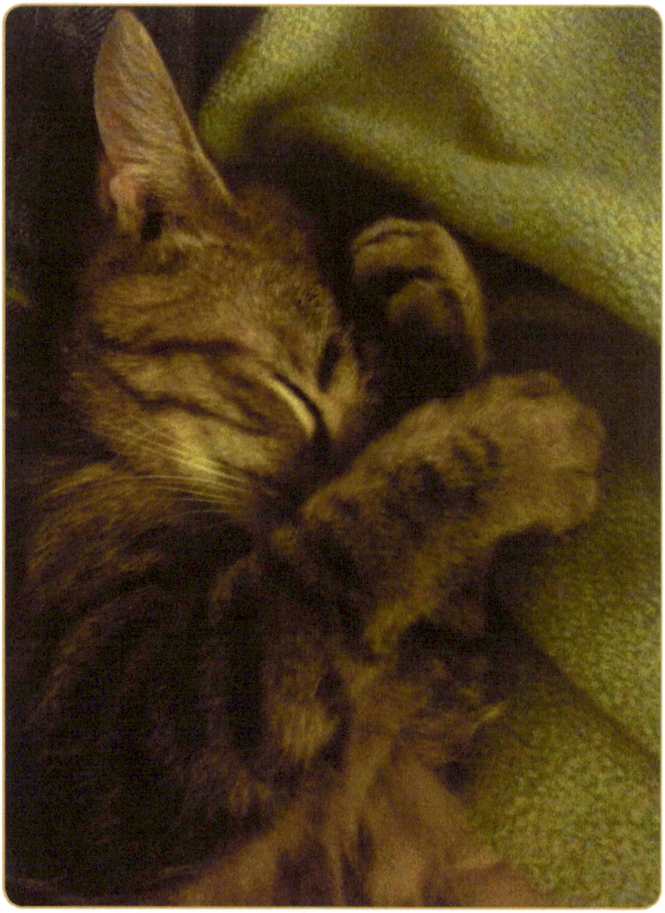

Anne Redmond McFarland

A kitten is more amusing than half
the people one is obliged to live with.

Lady Sydney Morgan, (1781–1859)

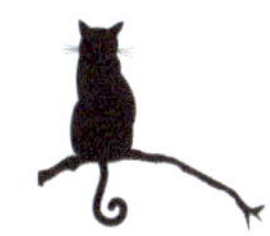

Gather kittens while you may,
Time brings only sorrow;
And the kittens of today
Will be old cats tomorrow.

Oliver Herford, (1863–1935)

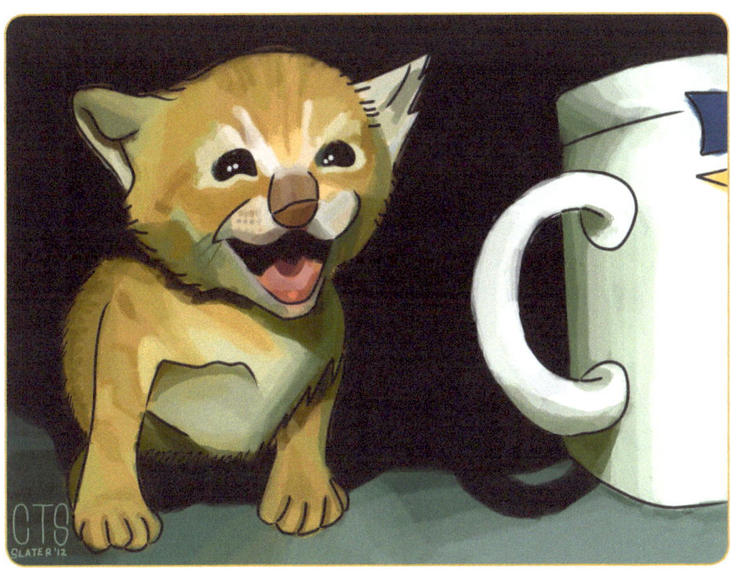

Cal Slater

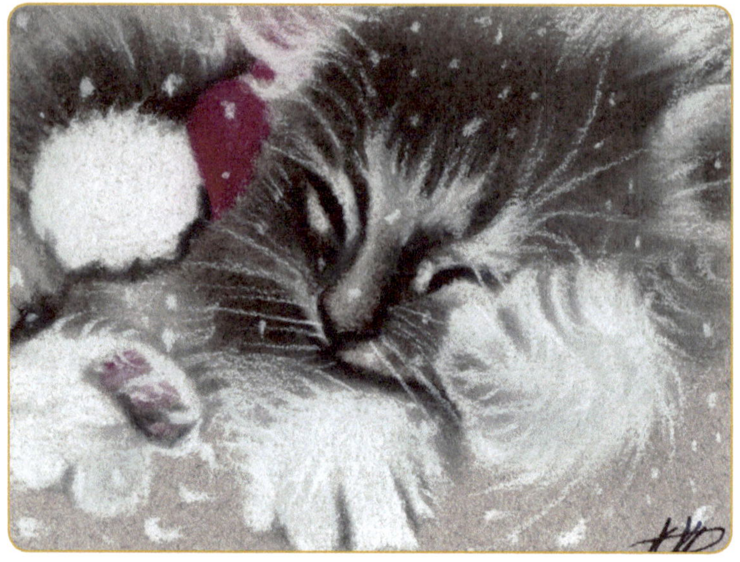

Katerina Koukiotis

A kitten is so flexible that she is almost
double; the hind parts are equivalent to
another kitten with which the forepart plays.
She does not discover that her tail
belongs to her until you tread on it.

Henry David Thoreau, (1817–1862)

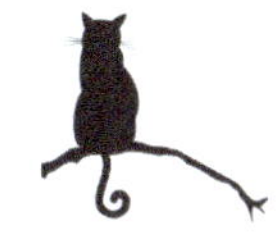

It is a very inconvenient habit of kittens (Alice had once made the remake) that, whatever you say to them, they always purr.

Lewis Carroll, (1832–1878)

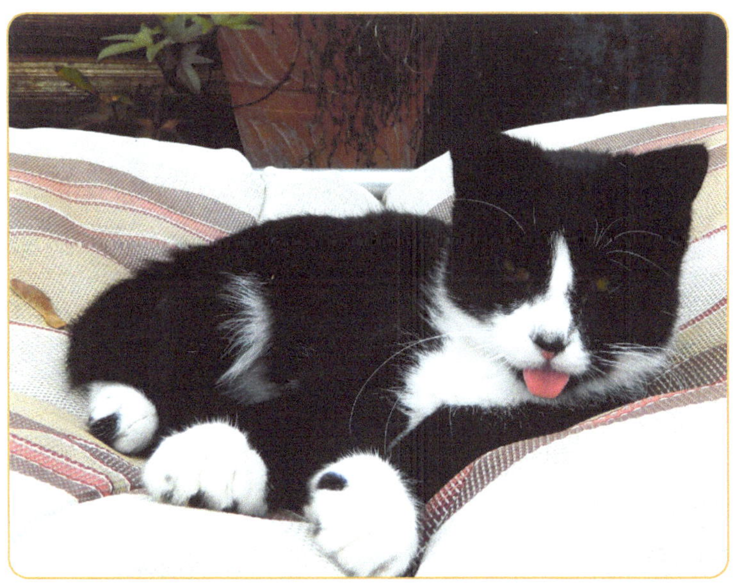

Grace Lipker

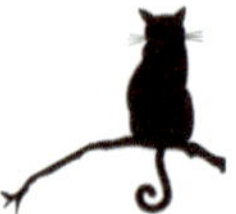

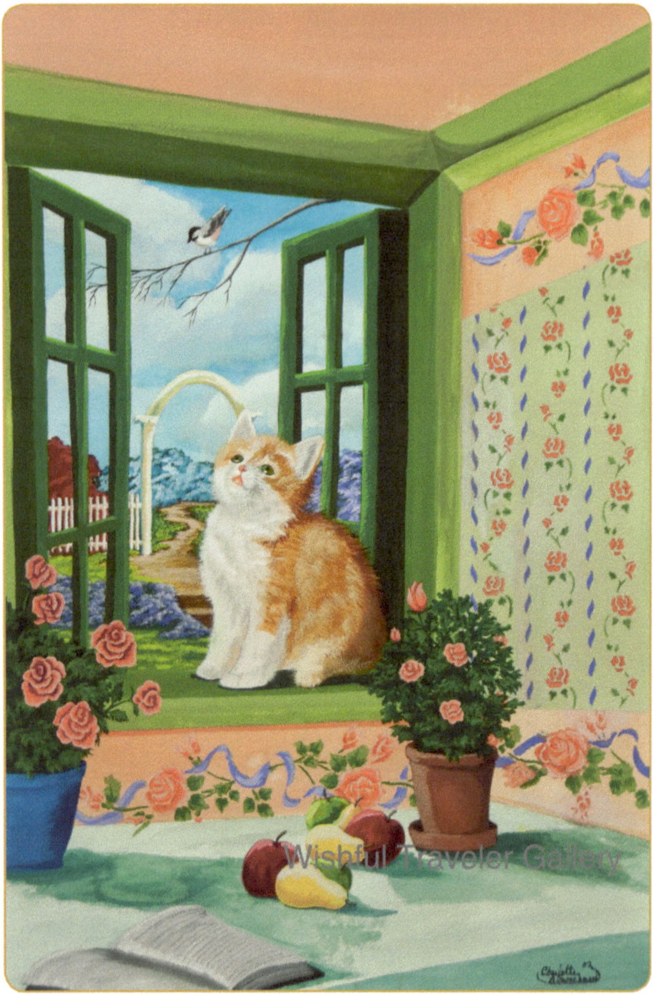

Charlotte Blanchard

There is no more intrepid explorer than a kitten.

Champfleury, (1820–1889)

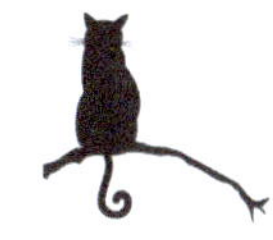

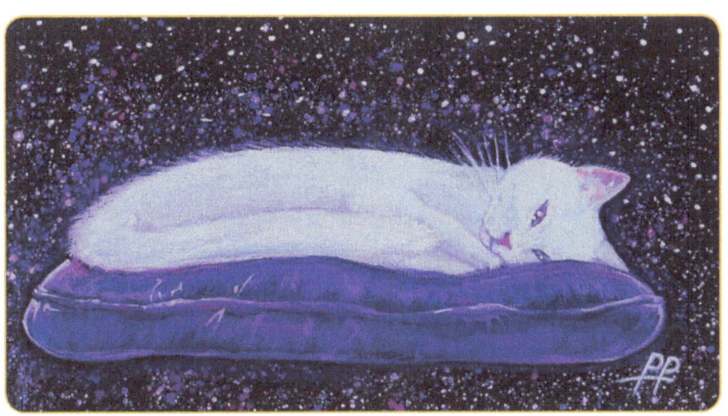

Penny Price

For the record, we all like men just as much as we like kittens. We even recognize that in certain situations, men are far superior. But while we'll accept baldness, bad table manners, even temporary sexual dysfunction, negative vibes toward cats get a new man quickly crossed off our list.

Cathryn Jakobson, (b. 1940)

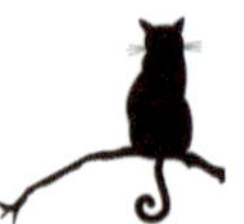

A child is a person who can't understand
why someone would give away
a perfectly good kitten.

Doug Larson (b. 1926)

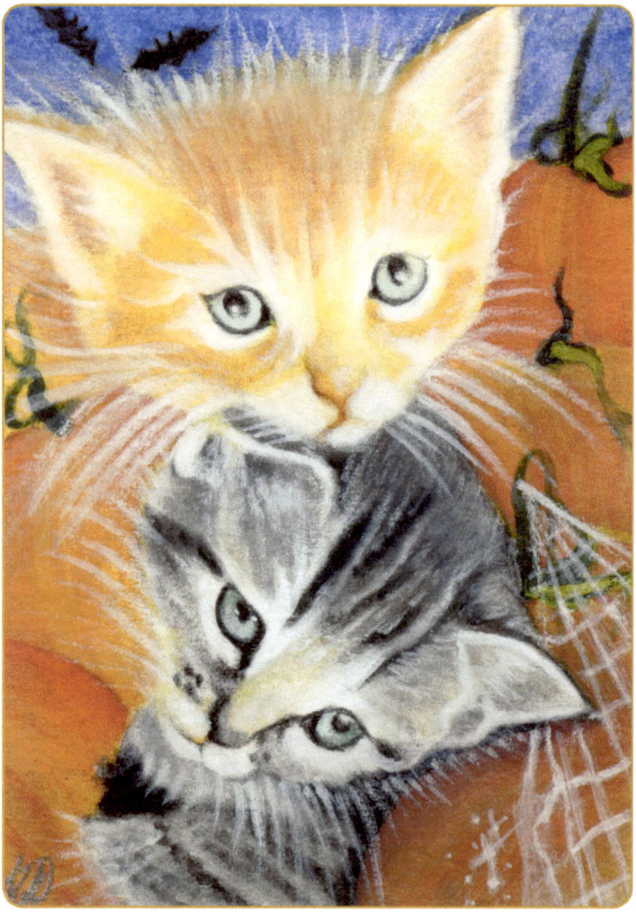

Katerina Koukiotis

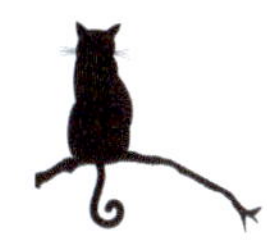

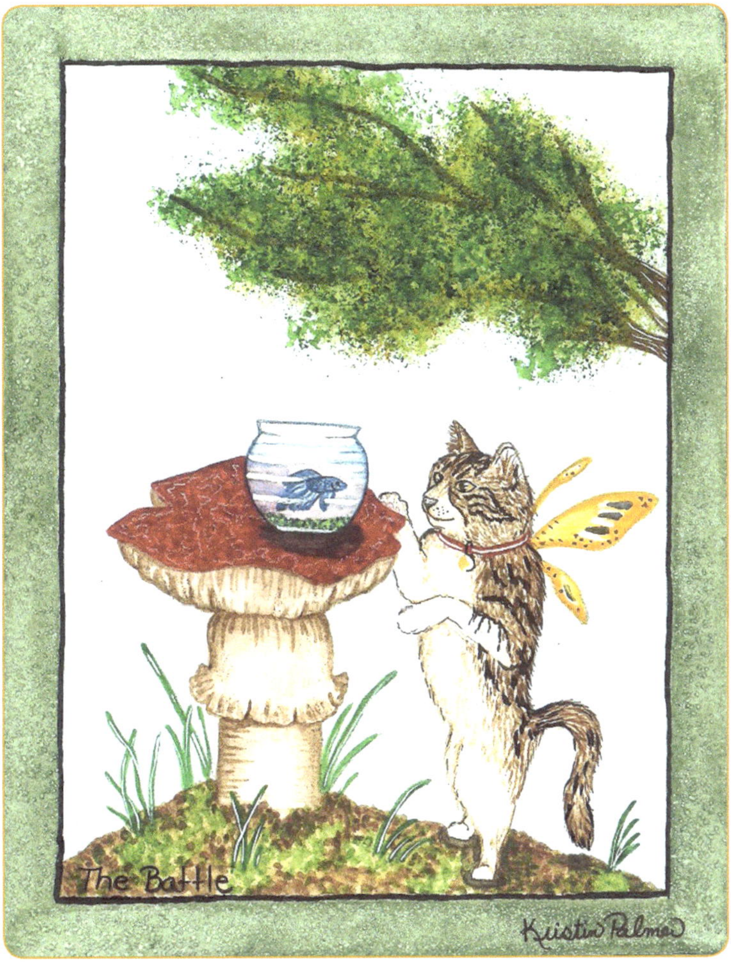

Kristin Palmer

But the kitten, how she starts,
Crouches, stretches, paws and darts!

William Wordsworth, (1770–1850)

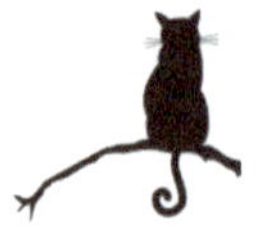

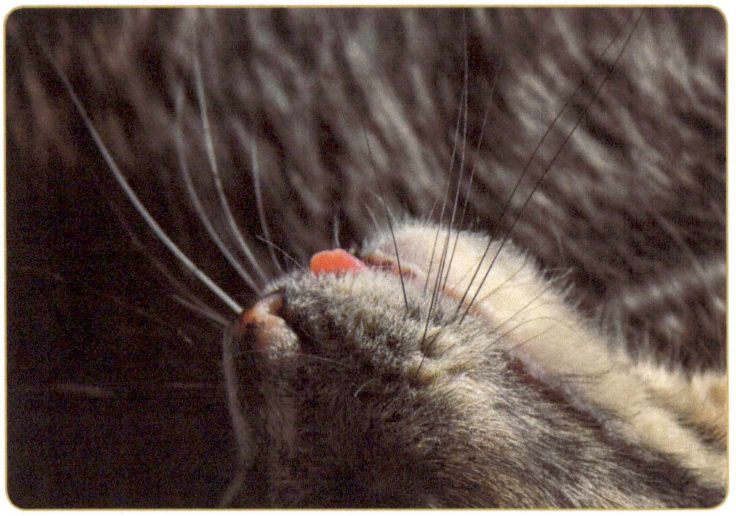

Susan Kordish

A kitten is the delight of a household.
All day long a comedy is played by
this incomparable actor.
Champfleury, (1820–1889)

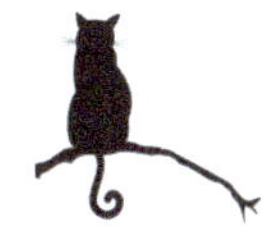

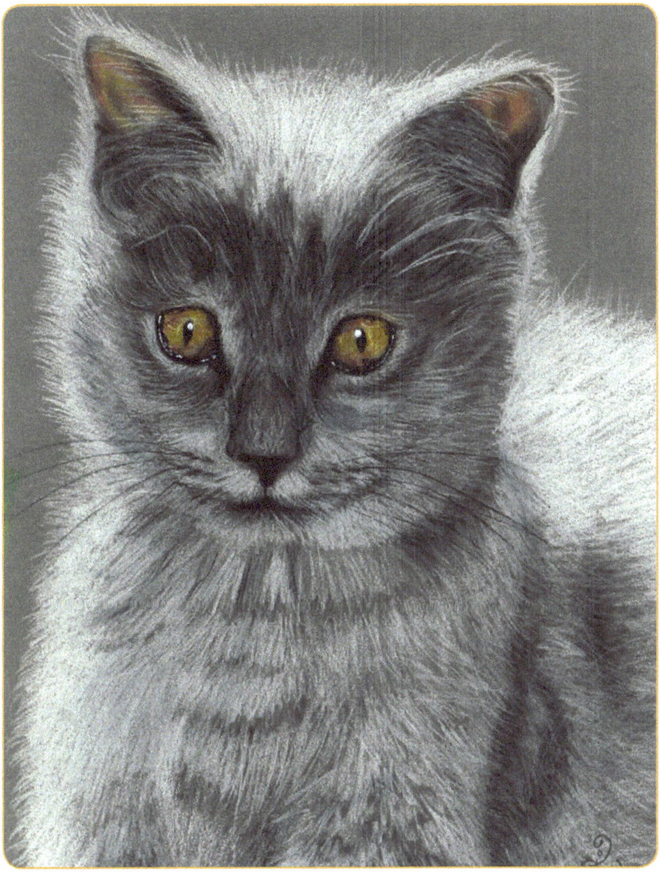

Tatjana Willms

A kitten is chiefly remarkable for rushing about like mad at nothing whatever, and generally stopping before it gets there.

Agnes Repplier, (1855–1950)

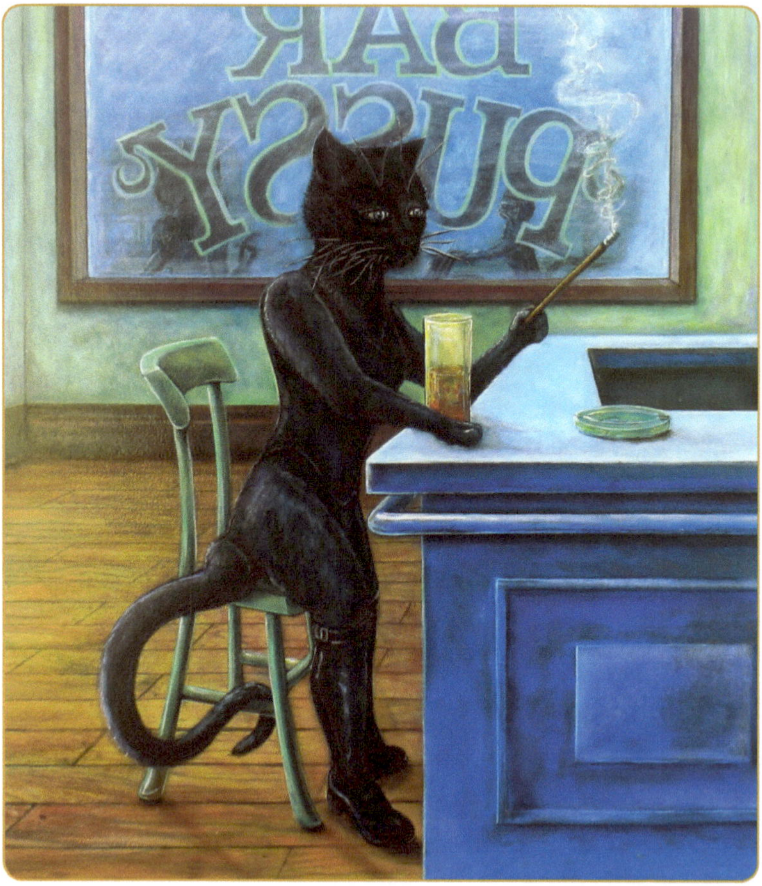

Penny Price

CHAPTER 4

Humor

A cat is a dilettante in fur.

Theophile Gautier, (1811–1872)

If a cat spoke, it would say things like "Hey, I don't see the problem here".

Roy Blount, Jr., (b. 1941)

Amazing products, cats. And real simple to manufacture.

Michael O'Donoghue, (1940–1994)

A black cat crossing your path signifies that the animal is going somewhere.

Grouch Marx, (1890–1977)

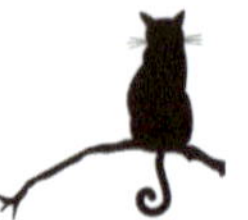

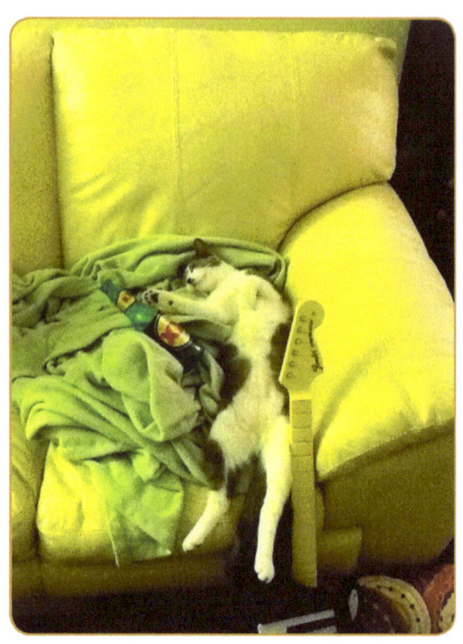

Anne Redmond McFarland

Cats do not need to be shown how to have a good time, for they are unfailingly ingenious in that respect.

James Mason, (1909–1984)

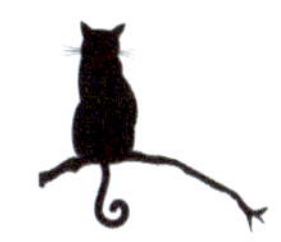

Show me a good mouser, and I'll show you a cat with bad breath.

Garfield cartoon personality

By Jim Davis, (b. 1945)

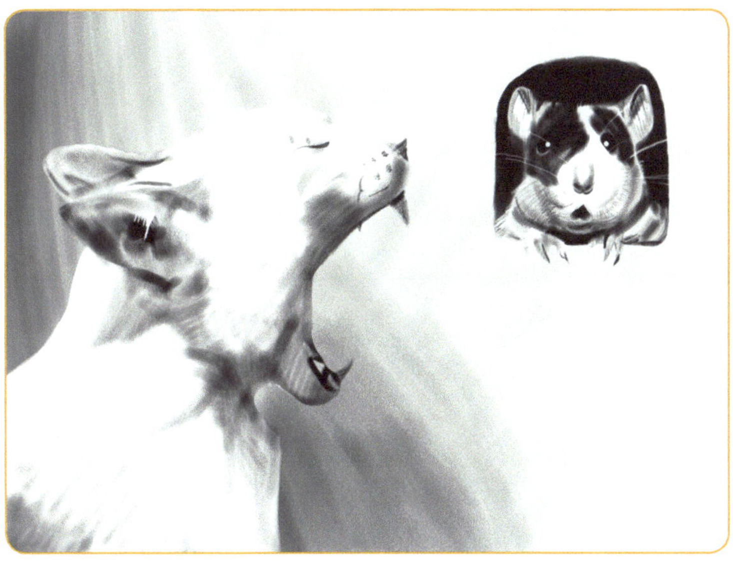

Cal Slater

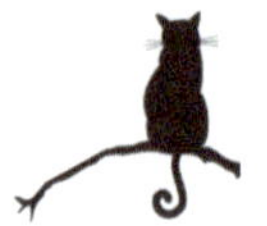

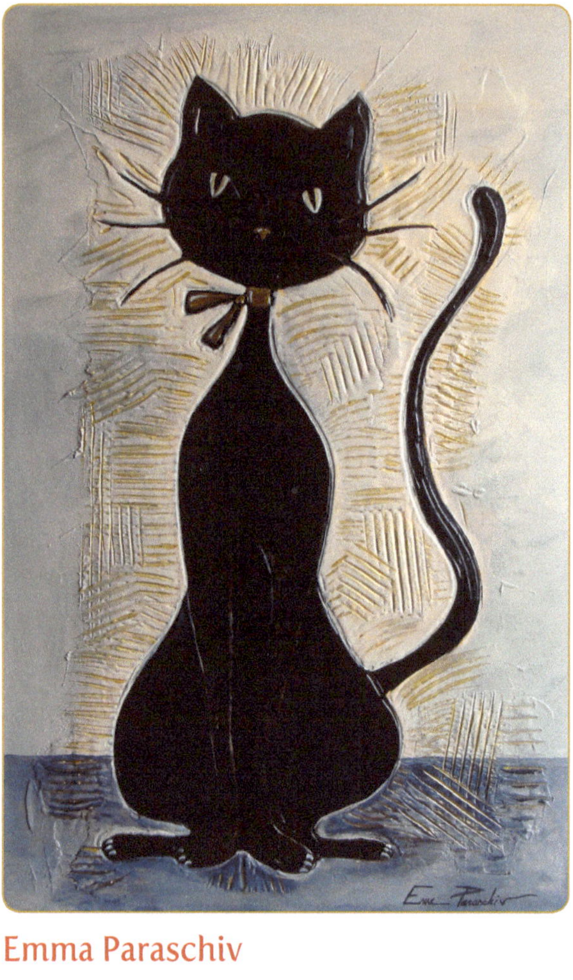

Emma Paraschiv

I have an Egyptian cat.
He leaves a pyramid in every room.
Rodney Dangerfield, (1921–2004)

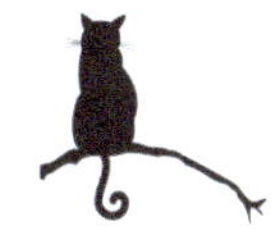

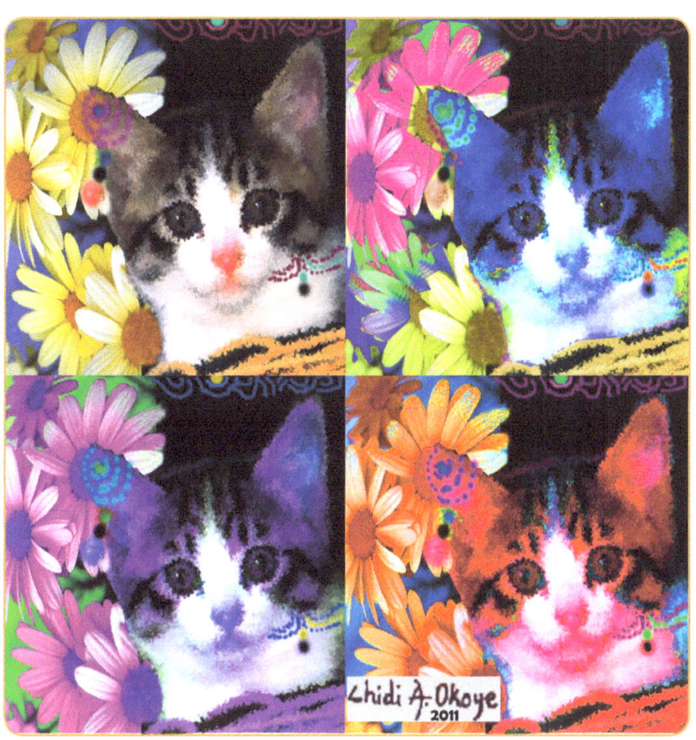

Childi A. Okoye

Two cats can live as cheaply as one, and their owner has twice as much fun.

Lloyd Alexander, (1924–2007)

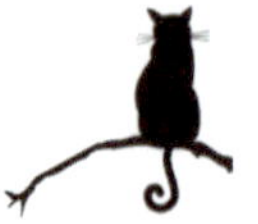

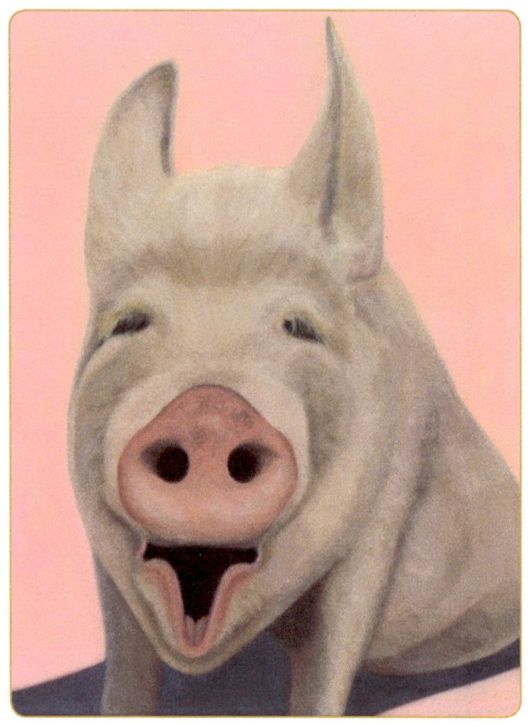

Dana Feagin

I like pigs. Dogs look up to us. Cats look down on us. Pigs treat us as equals.

Sir Winston Churchill, (1874–1965)

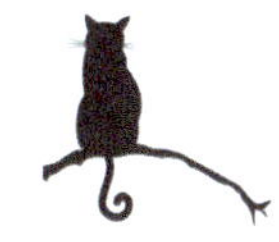

Caesar and I kind of hit adolescence together. It is not an era of neutering, so Caesar walks on the wild side. While I engage in hours of tongue kissing and heavy petting he goes out and gets laid.

Julia Phillips, (1944–2002)

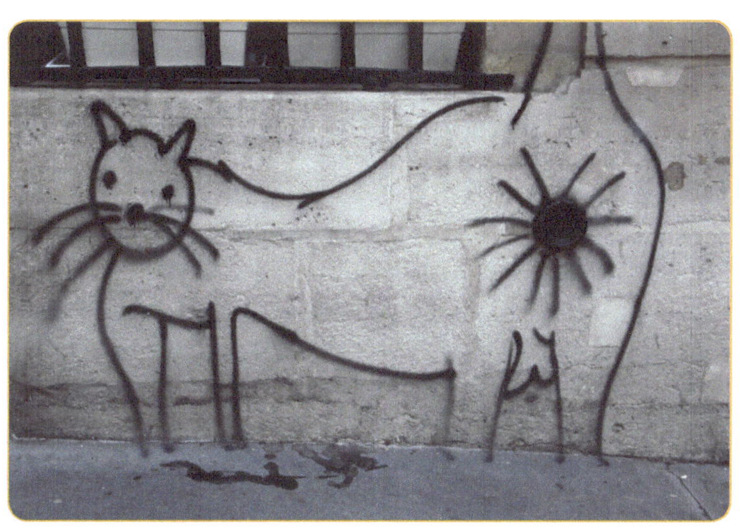

Antonino Falleti

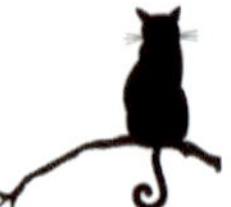

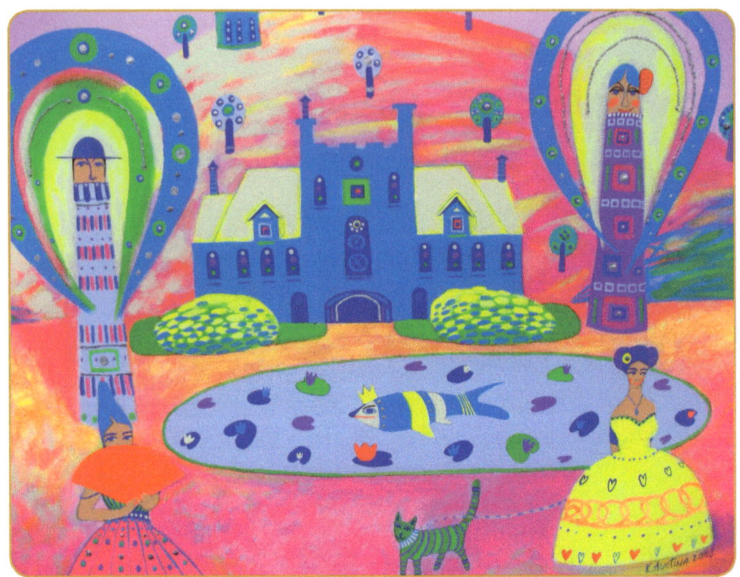

Katrina Avotina

So it is, and such is life. The cat's away, and the mice they play.

Charles Dickens, (1812–1870)

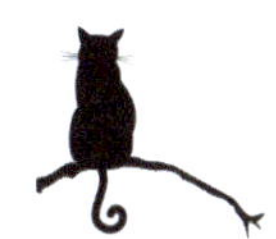

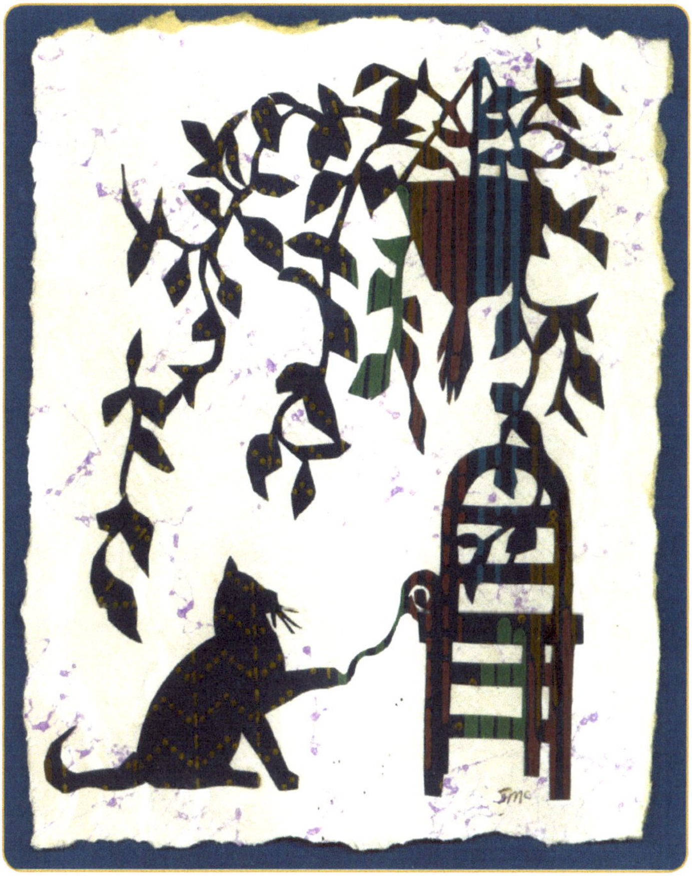

Sue McNulty

Whenever we heard a crash in the other room, one of us would say "There's a reason the first three letters of 'catastrophe' are C-A-T!"

St. James Shatzer, (b. 1950)

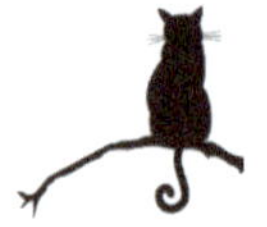

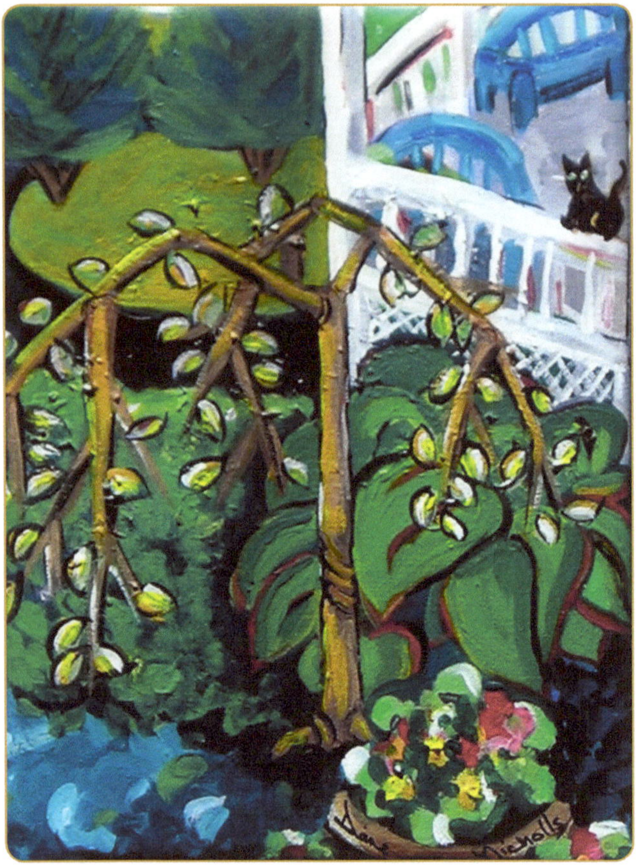

Diane Nicholls

Did St. Francis preach to the birds?
Whatever for? If he really liked birds he
would have done better to preach to the cats.

Rebecca West, (1892–1983)

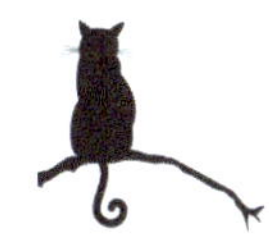

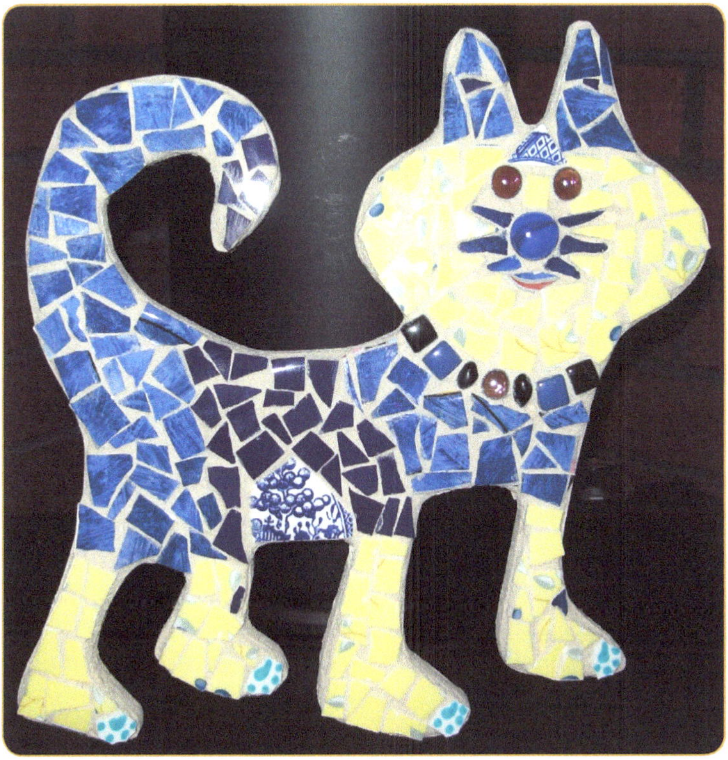

Traci Hallstrom

They say a cat always lands on his feet, but they don't mention the pain.

Garfield, cartoon personality by Jim Davis, (b. 1945)

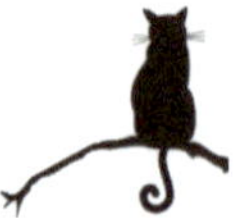

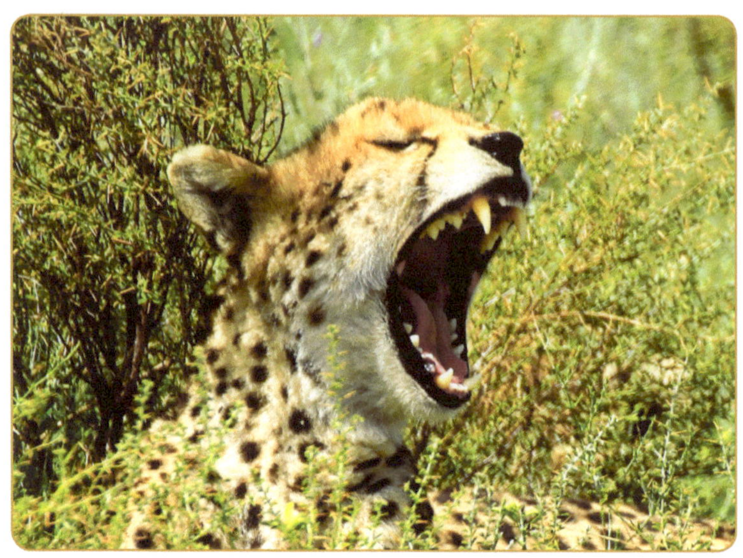

Roland Anderson

He who laugheth too much hath the nature of a fool; he that laugheth not at all hath the nature of an old cat.

Thomas Fuller I, (1907–1988)

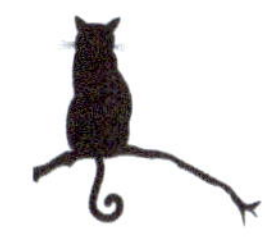

Never try to outstubborn a cat.

Robert A. Heinlein, (1907–1968)

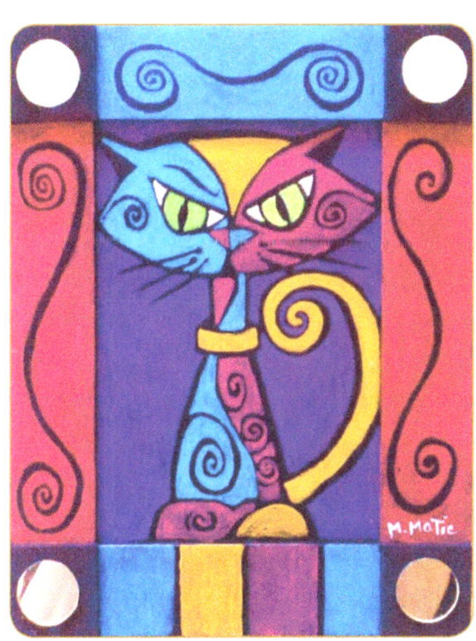

Milena Matic

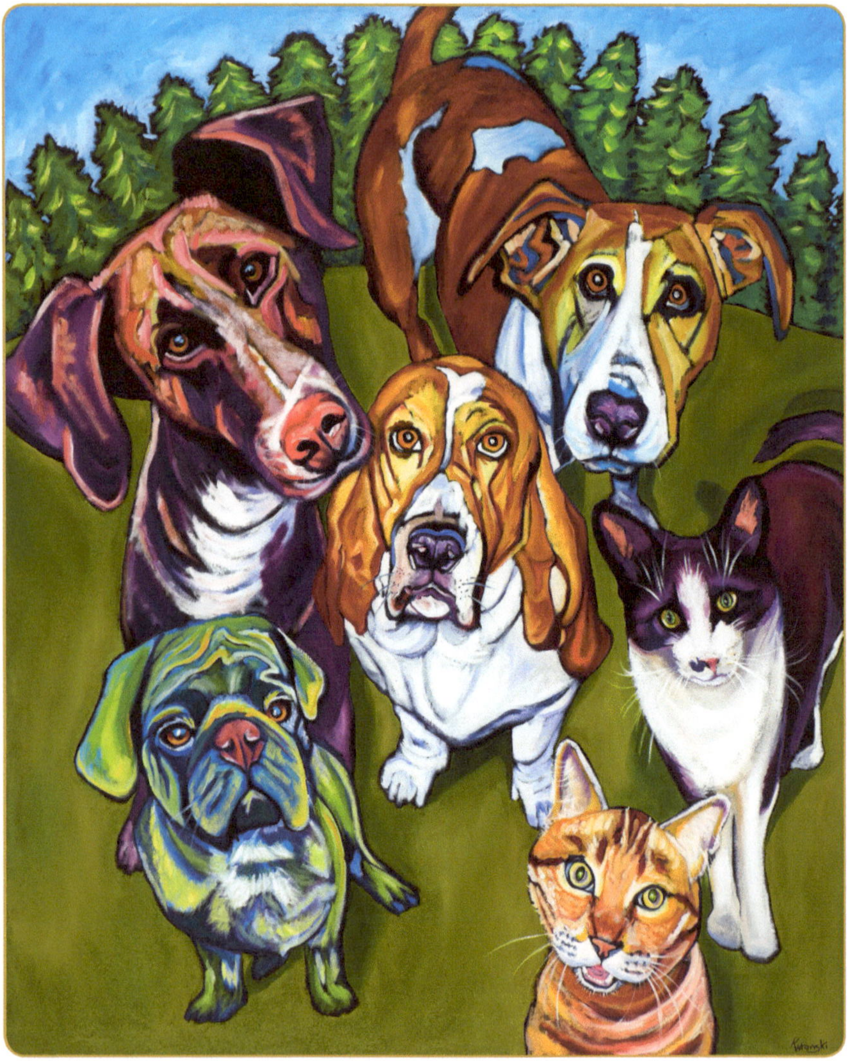

Kathryn Wronski

CHAPTER 5

Of Cats & Dogs

To Someone Very Good and Just,
Who has proved worthy of her trust,
A Cat will sometimes condescend—
The Dog is Everybody's Friend.
Oliver Herford, (1863–1935)

A dog is prose, a cat is a poem.
Jean Burden, (1914–2008)

Let Hercules himself do what he may,
The cat will mew and dog will have his day.
William Shakespeare, (1564–1616)

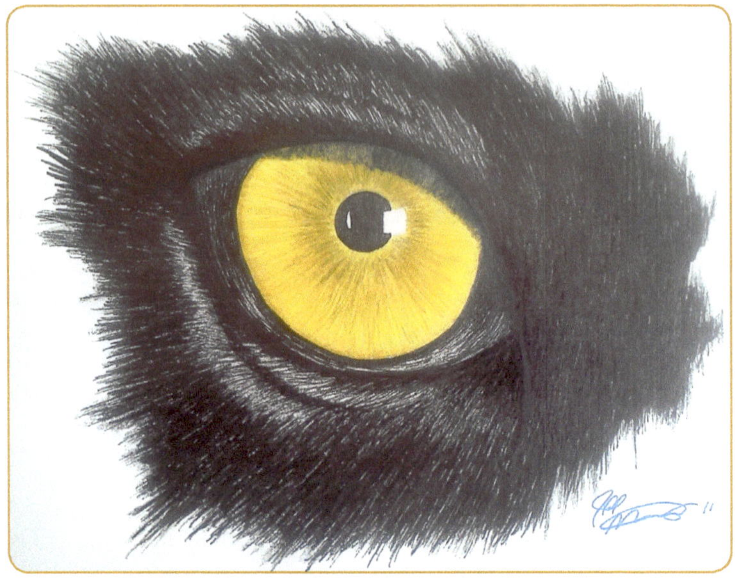

Jeff Montagne

A dog wears his insides on his outside, writ large and plain. A cat thinks at the back of its head, and the results can surprise you. No wonder cats were burned as witches; it hurts people's feelings not to know what the lower orders are up to.

Barbara Holland, (1933–2010)

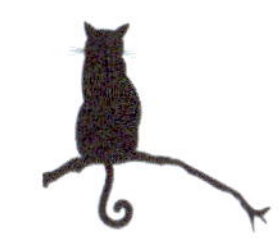

A dog is like a liberal. He wants to please everybody. A cat really doesn't need to know that everybody loves him.

William Kunstler, (1919–1995)

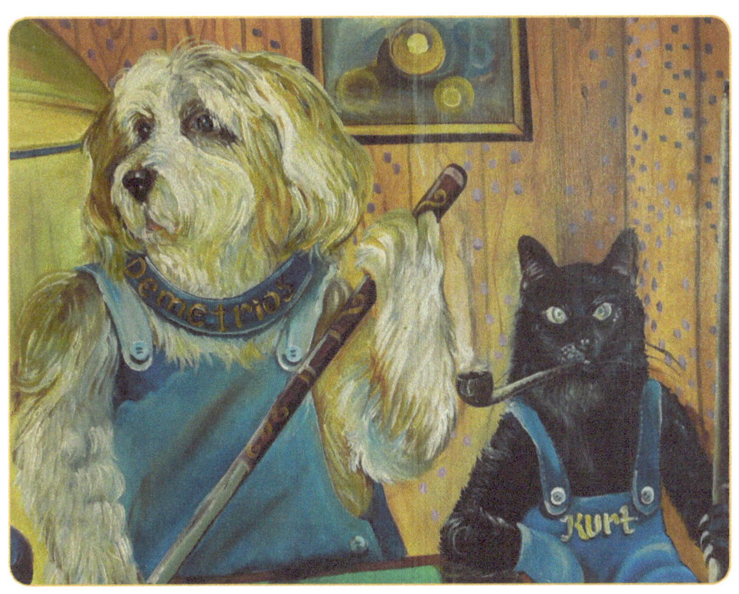

Linda Rufo

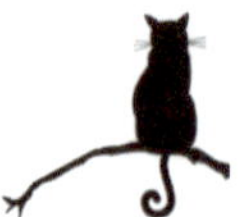

By and large, people who enjoy teaching animals to roll over will find themselves happier with a dog.

Barbara Holland, (1933–2010)

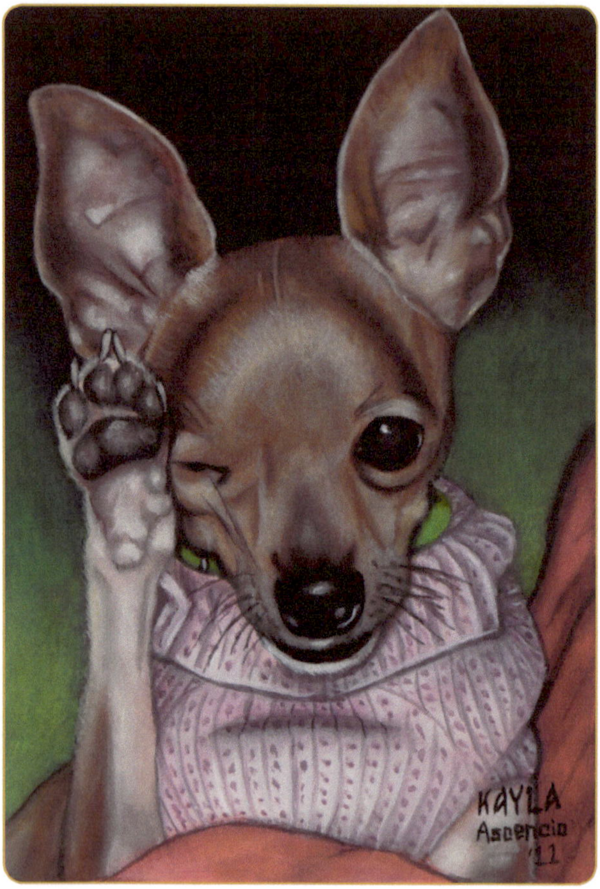

Kayla Ascencio

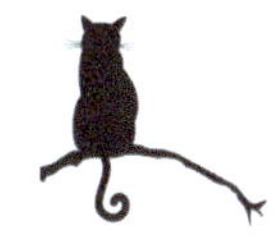

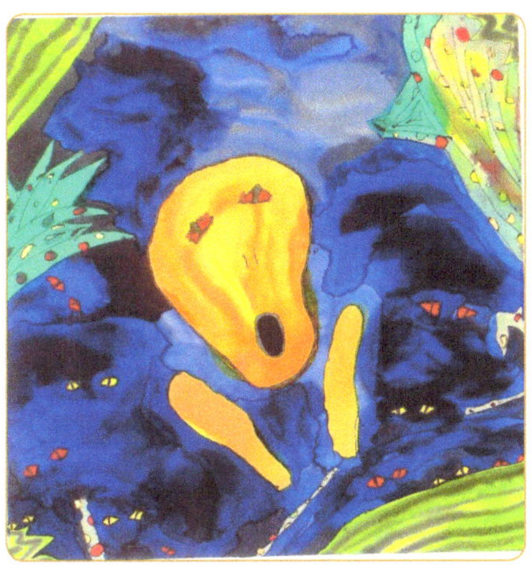

Lior Immanuel Fisher

If animals could speak, the dog would be a blundering, outspoken, honest fellow—but the cat would have the rare grace of never saying a word too much.

Philip G. Hamerton, (1834–1894)

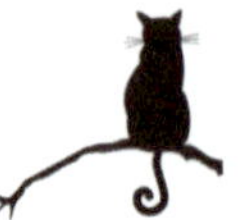

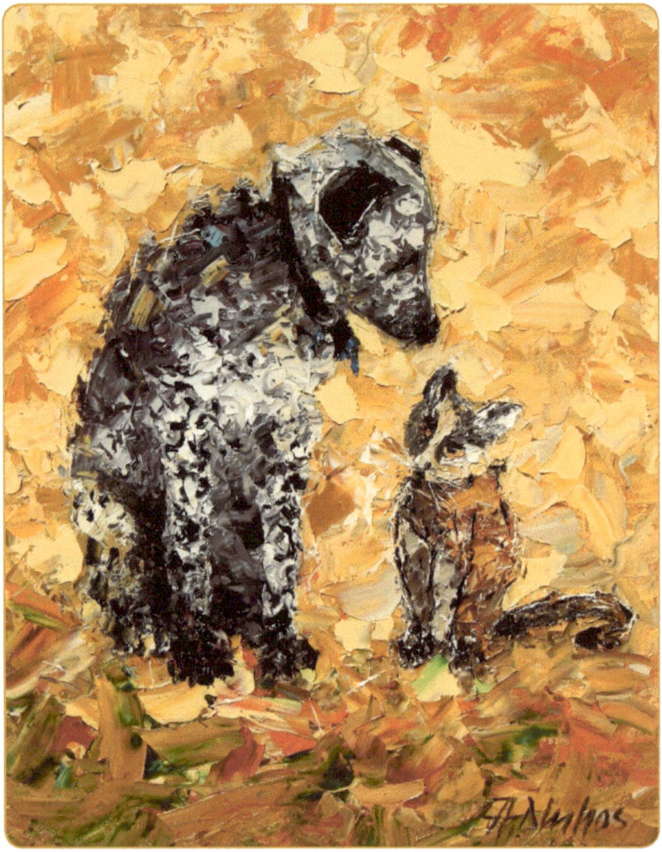

Andre Dluhos

Dogs instinctively realize that cats are smarter than they are, so they resent the intrusion of a cat upon the household.

Eric Gurney, (1910–1992)

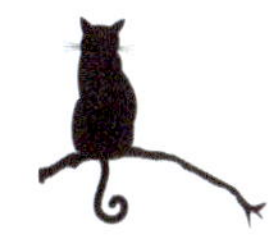

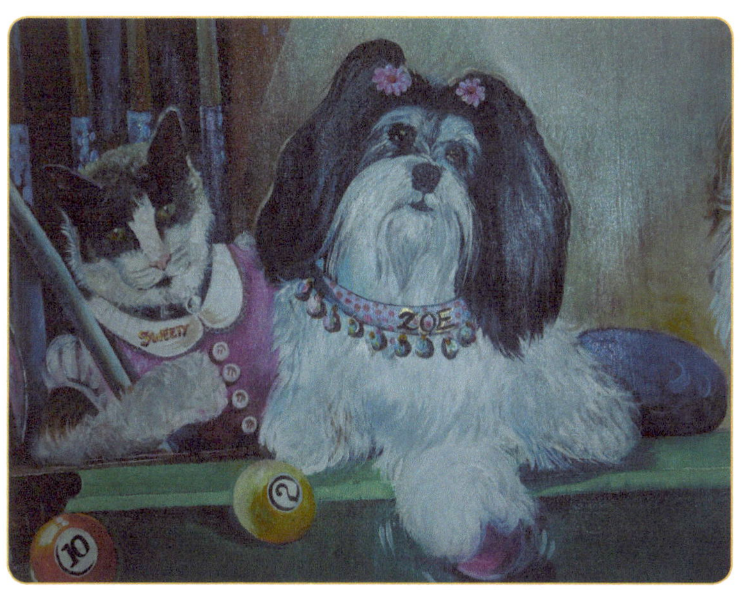

Linda Rufo

Artist like cats; soldiers like dogs.
Desmond Morris, (b. 1928)

Again I must remind you that
A Dog's a Dog—A CAT"S A CAT.
T.S. Eliot, (1888–1965)

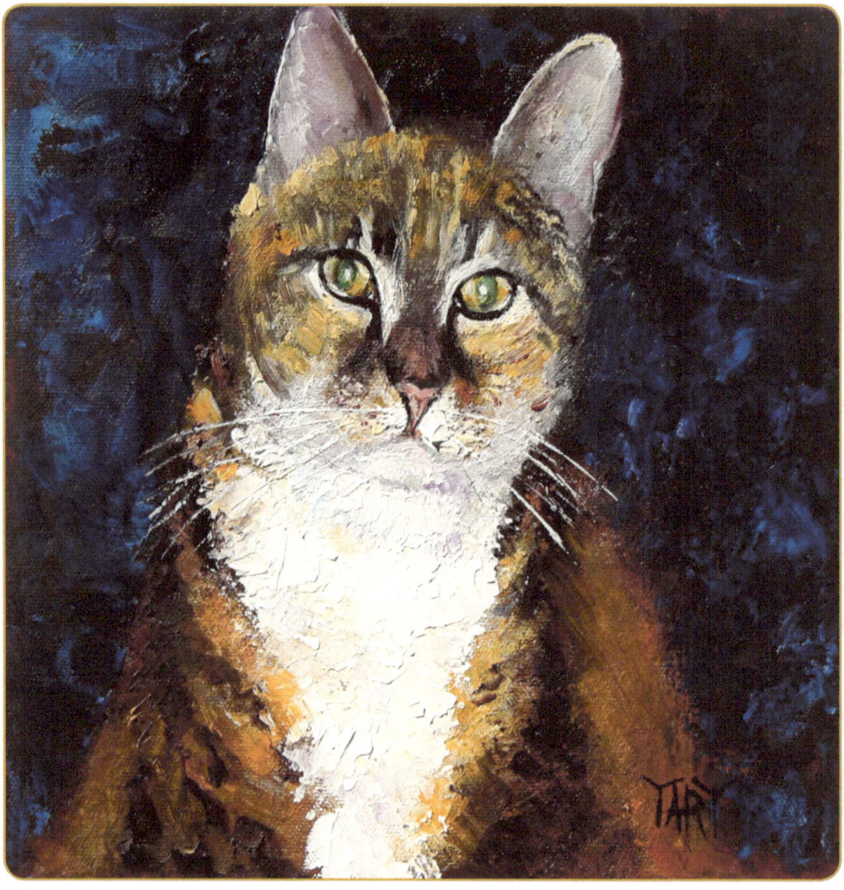

Yary Dluhos

CHAPTER 6

The Cat Personality

Cats know how to obtain food
without labor, shelter without confinement,
and love without penalties.
W. L. George, (b. 1928)

Cats seem to go on the principle that it never
does any harm to ask for what you want.
Joseph Wood Krutch, (1893–1970)

Cats are a mysterious kind of folk. There is more
passing in their minds than we are aware of.
Sir Walter Scott, (1771–1832)

The cat is, above all things, a dramatist.
Margaret Benson, (1865–1916)

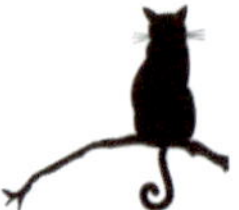

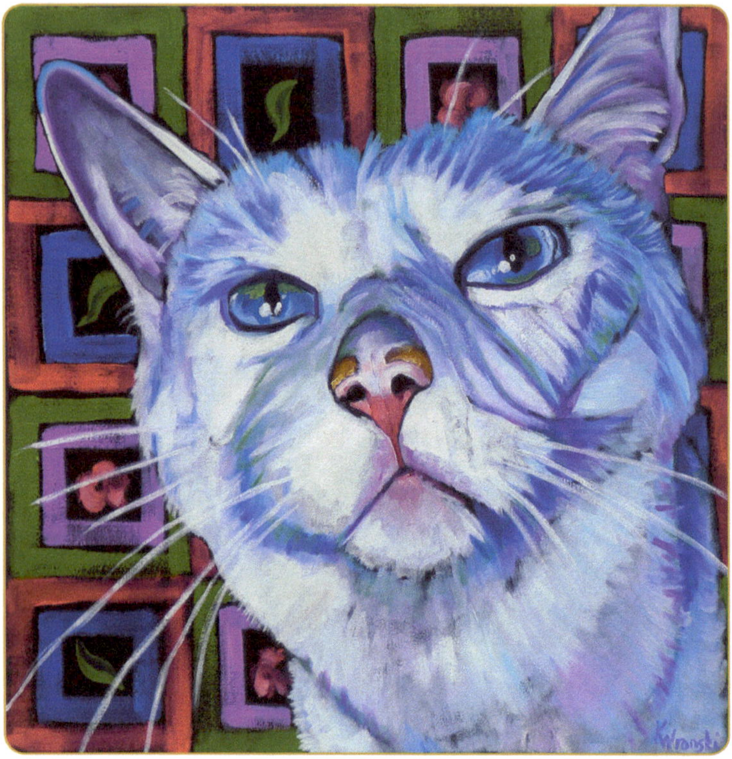

Kathryn Wronski

Who can believe that there is no soul
behind those luminous eyes!
Theophile Gautier, (1811–1872)

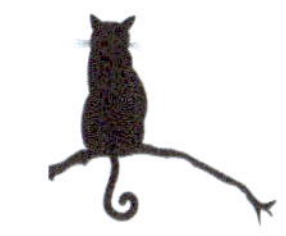

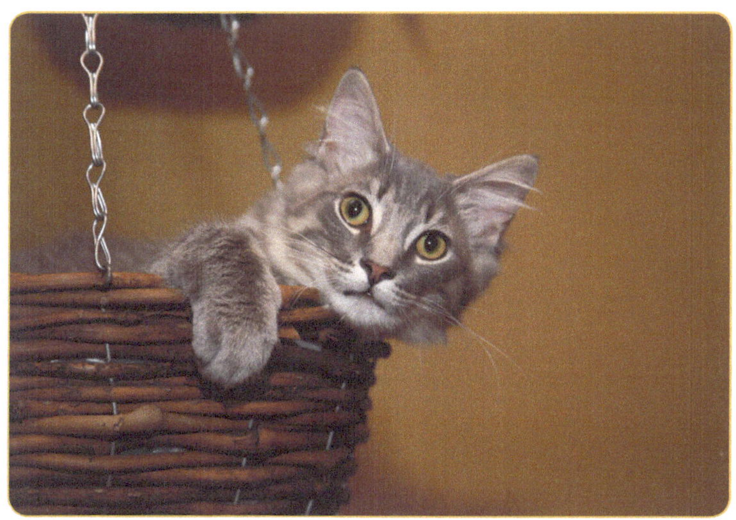

Gene Gissin

Of all domestic animals the cat is the most expressive. His face is capable of showing a wide range of expressions. His tail is a mirror of his mind. His gracefulness is surpassed only by his agility.

Walter Chandoha, (b. 1920)

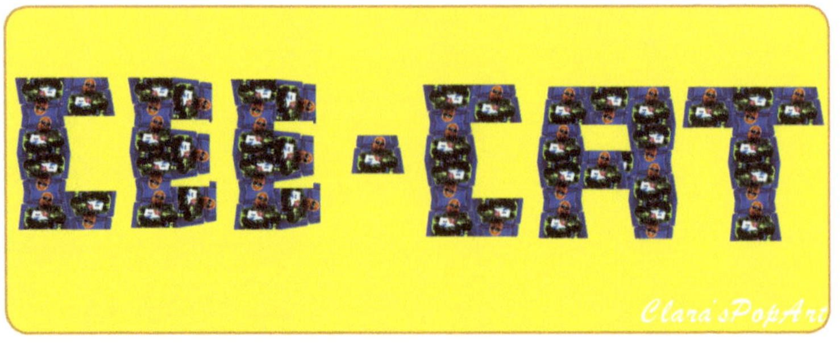

Clara Milleret Germanotta

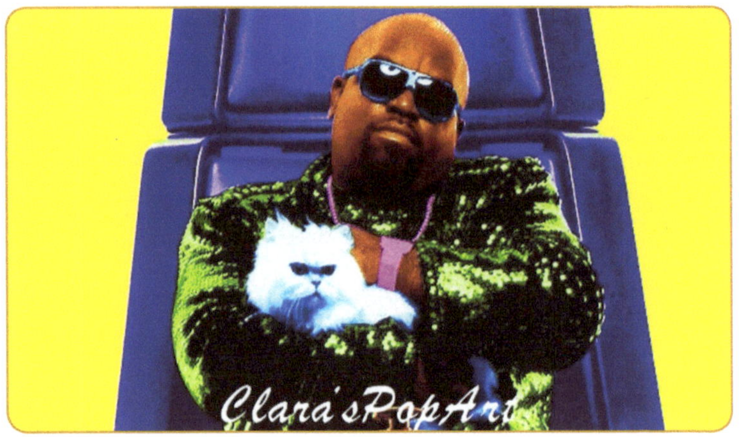

Clara Milleret Germanotta

Meow is like aloha—it can mean anything.
Hank Ketchum, (1920–2001)

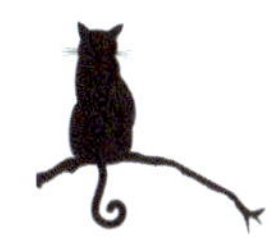

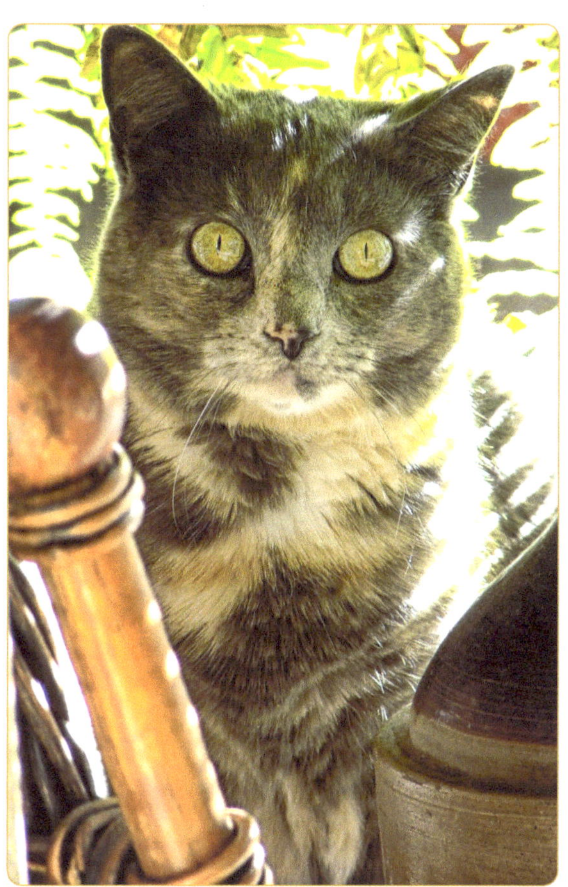

Susan Kordish

Cats always know whether people like or dislike them. They do not always care enough to do anything about it.

Winifred Carriere, (1912–2002)

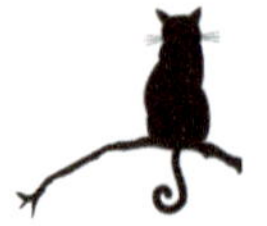

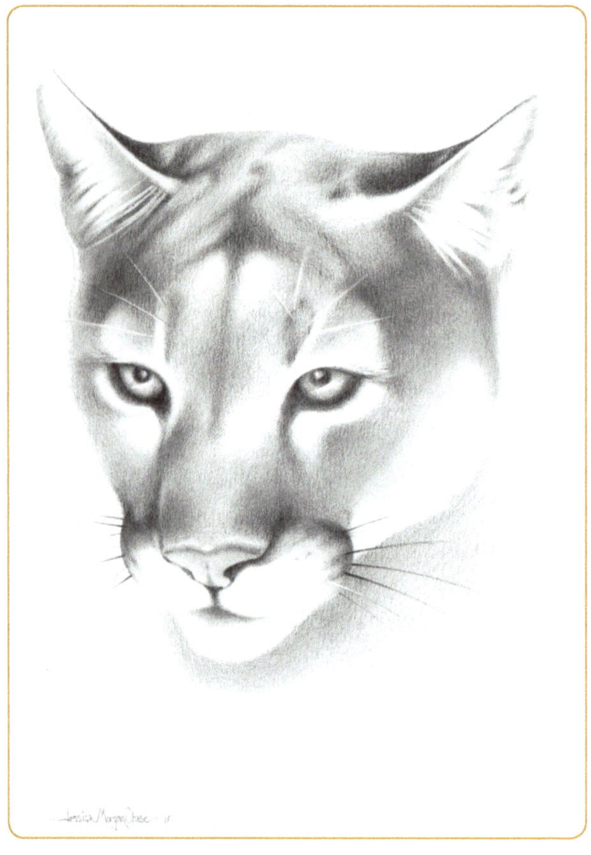

Jessica Morgan-Chase

Night and day in gentleness or cruelty, for better or for worse, no other animal is as much of an extremist as the cat.

Fernand Mery, (1897–1984)

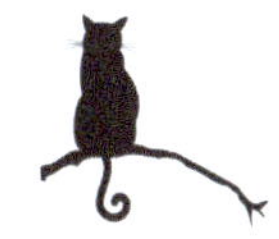

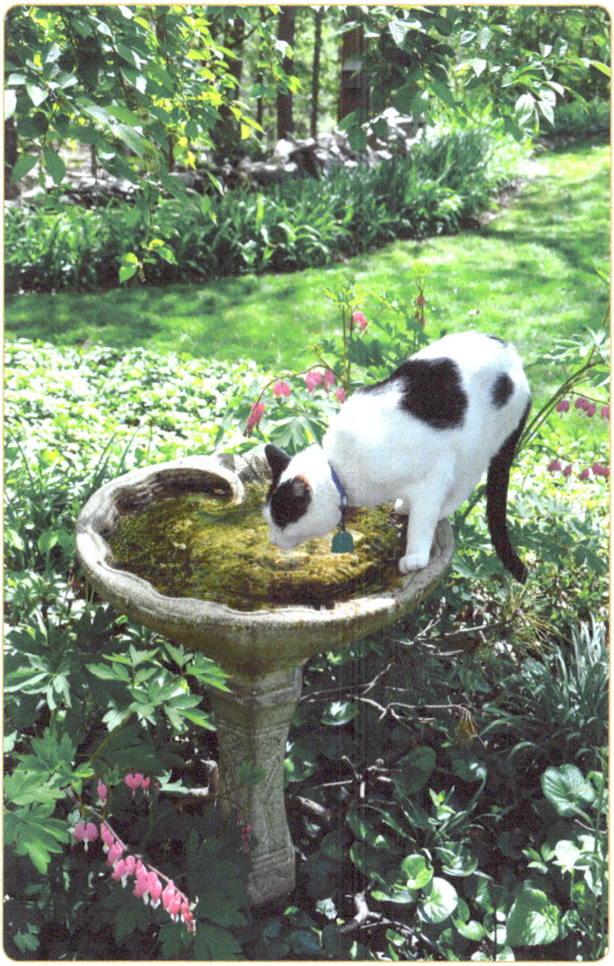

Nancy Howard

Most cats have trained their owners.

Leon F. Whitney, (1894–1973)

Cats refuse to take the blame got anything—including their own sins.

Elizabeth Peters, (b. 1927)

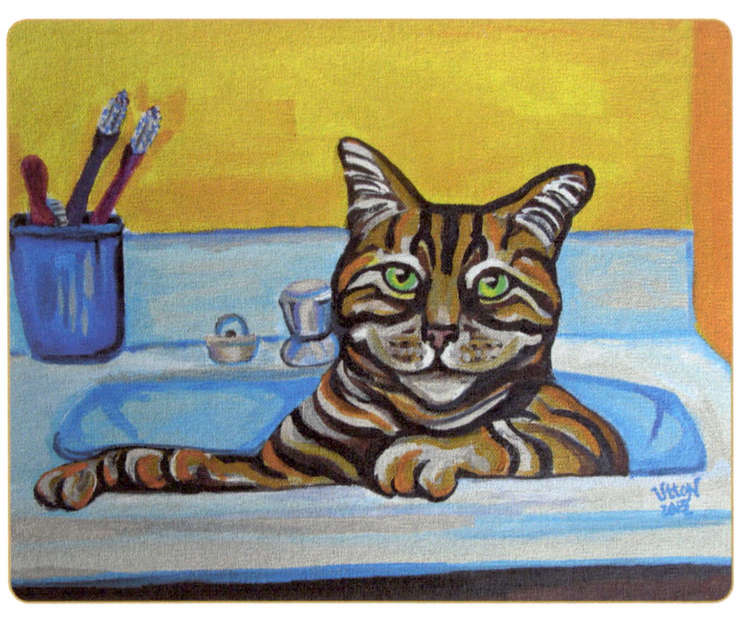

Pamela Utton

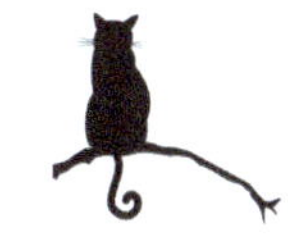

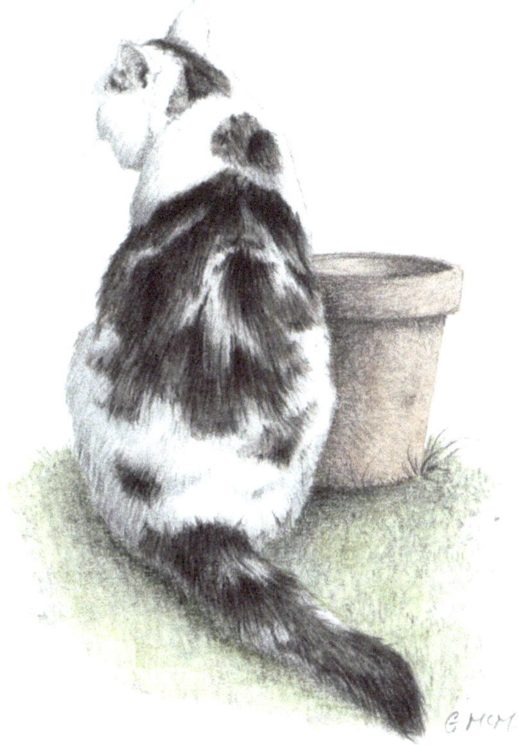

Gillian McMurry

To understand a cat, you must realize that he has his own gifts, his own viewpoint, even his own morality.

Lilian Jackson Braun, (1913–2011)

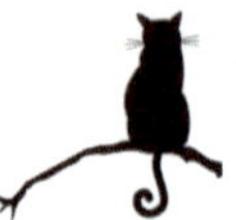

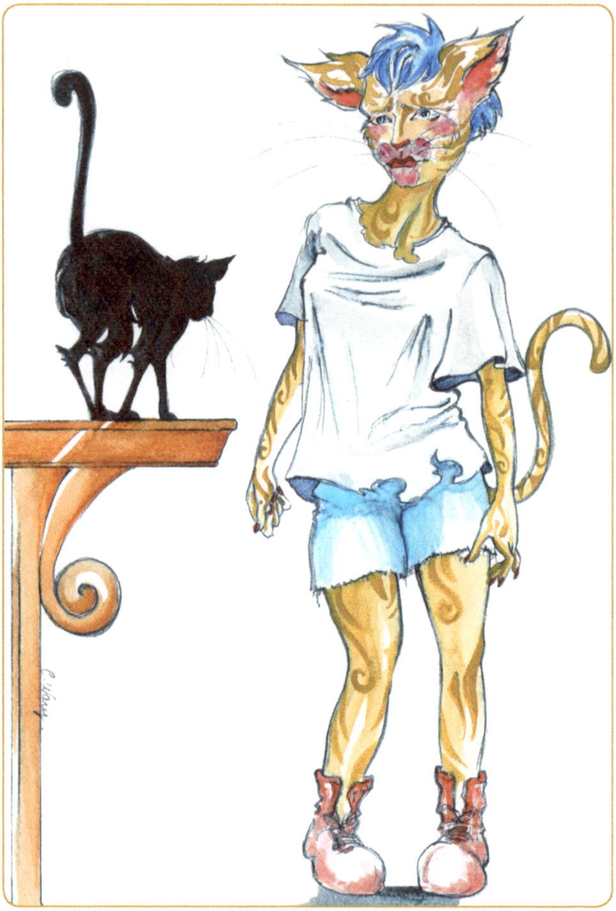

Chloé Wary

It always gives me a shiver when I see
a cat seeing what I can't see.

Eleanor Farjeon, (1881–1965)

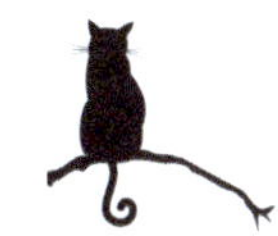

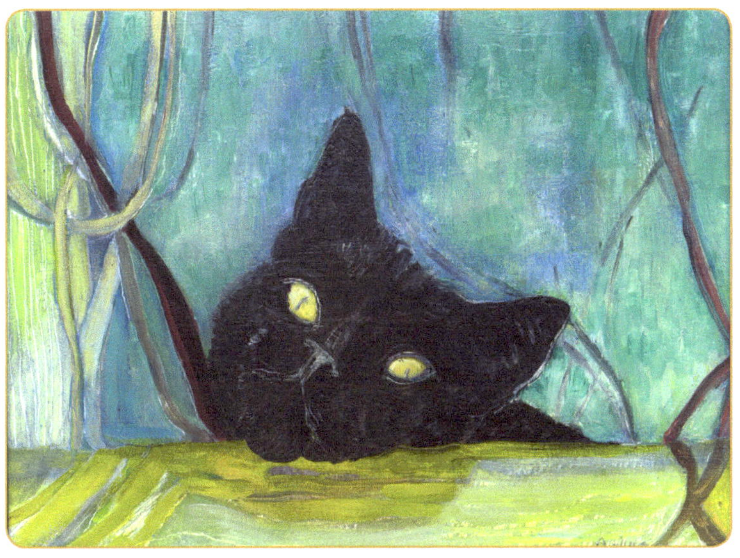

Quinne Fokes

Purring would seem to be, in her case,
an automatic safety-valve device for dealing
with happiness overflow.

Monica Edwards, (1912–1998)

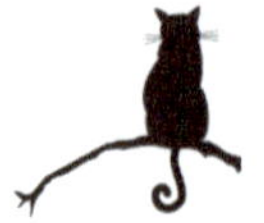

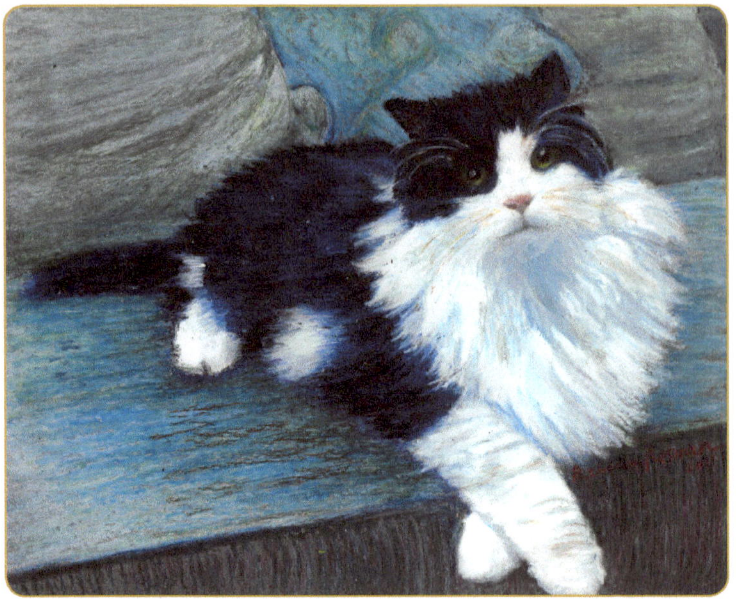

Rebecca Rosman

A cat pours his body on the floor like water.
It is restful just to see him.
William Lyon Phelps, (1865–1943)

You can't look at a sleeping cat and feel tense.
Jane Pauley, (b. 1950)

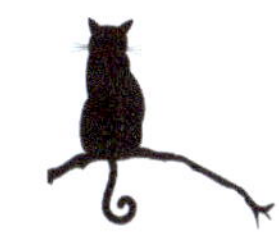

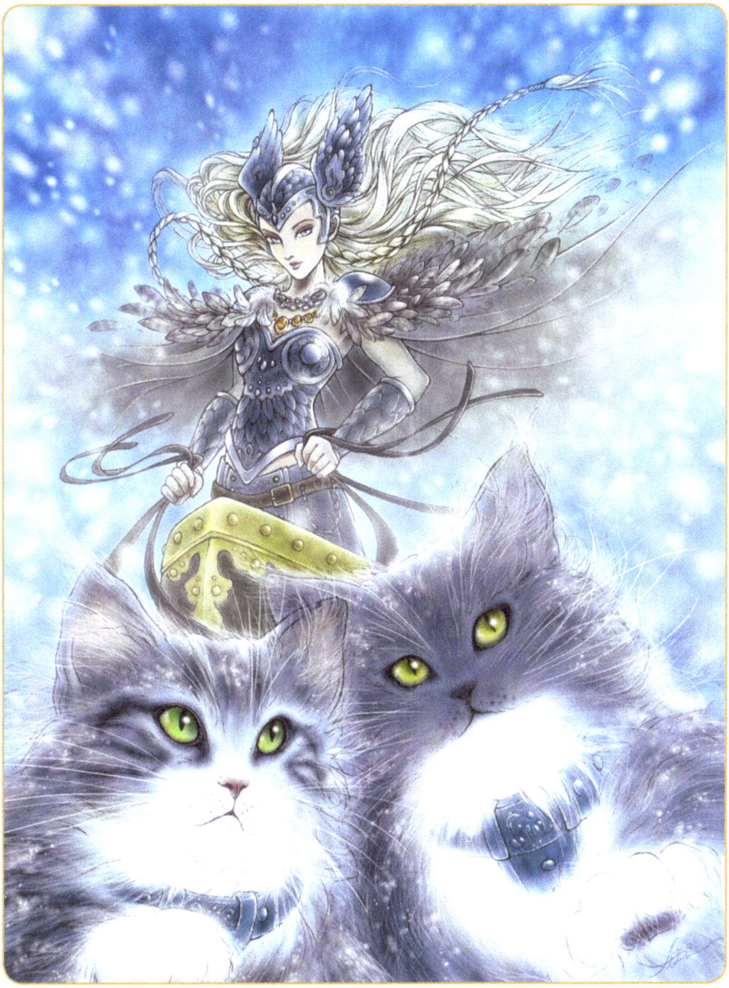

CHAPTER 6

The Cat Personality

Mitzi Sato-Wluff

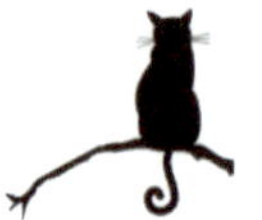

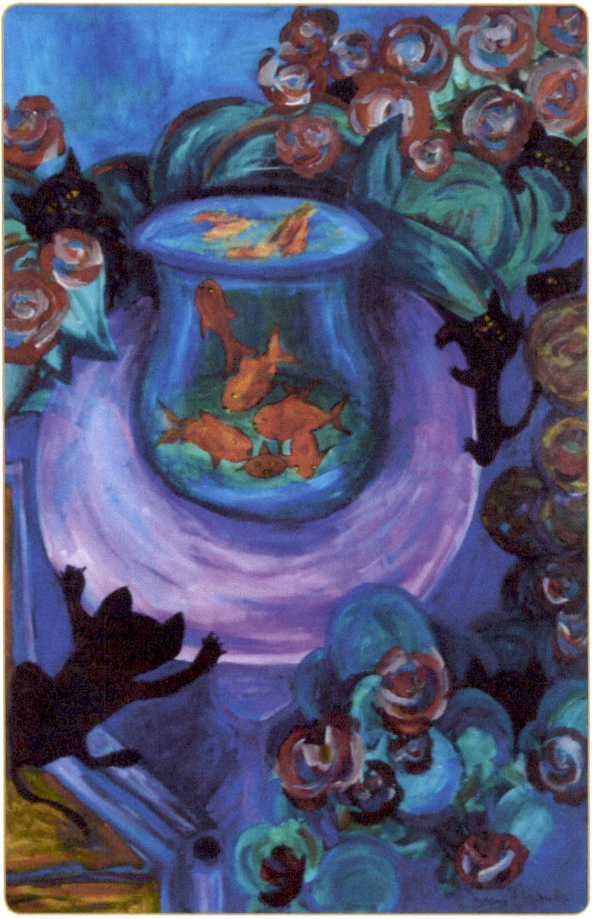

Diane Nicholls

Where food was concerned Charles,
like all cats, was an incorrigible thief.

Michael Joseph, (1914–1981)

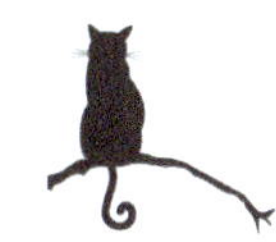

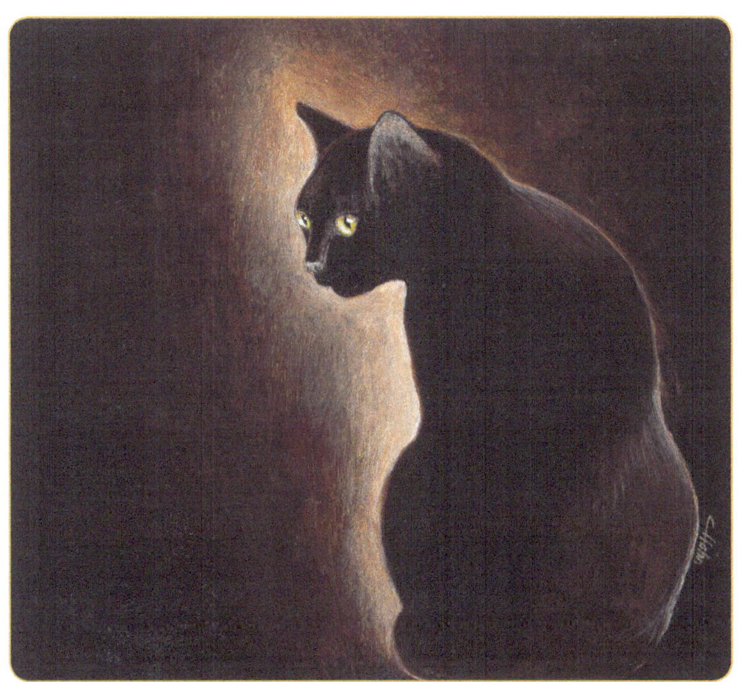

Claudia Hahn

He seems the incarnation of everything soft and silky and velvety, without a sharp edge in his composition, a dreamer whose philosophy is sleep and let sleep . . .

Hector Hugh Munro (Saki), (1870–1916)

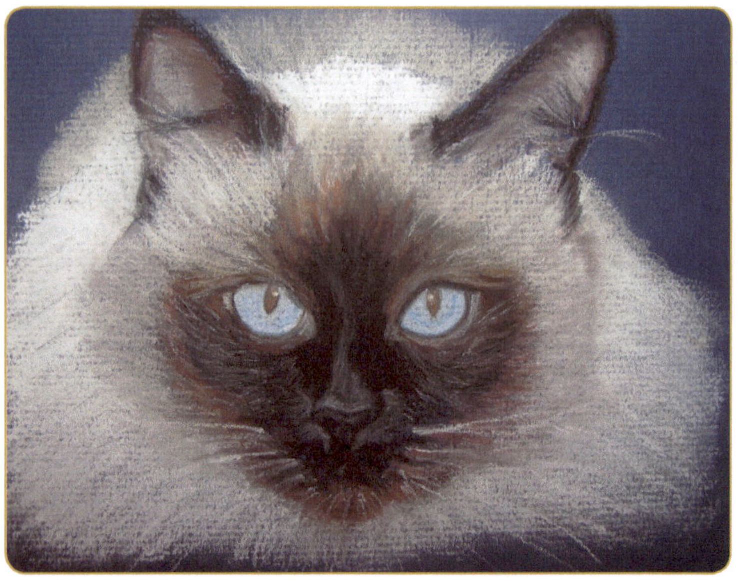

Melissa Crow

When a Cat adopts you there is nothing to be done about it except to put up with it and wait until the wind changes.

T. S. Eliot, (1888–1965)

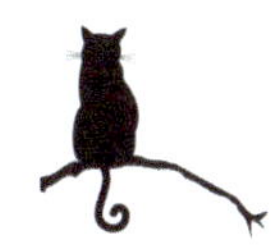

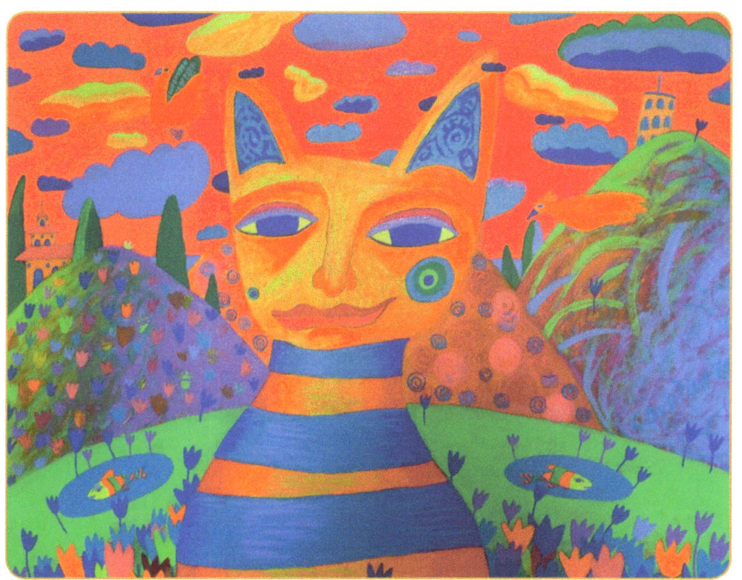

Katrina Avotina

A cat is more intelligent than people believe
and can be taught any crime.

Mark Twain, (1835–1910)

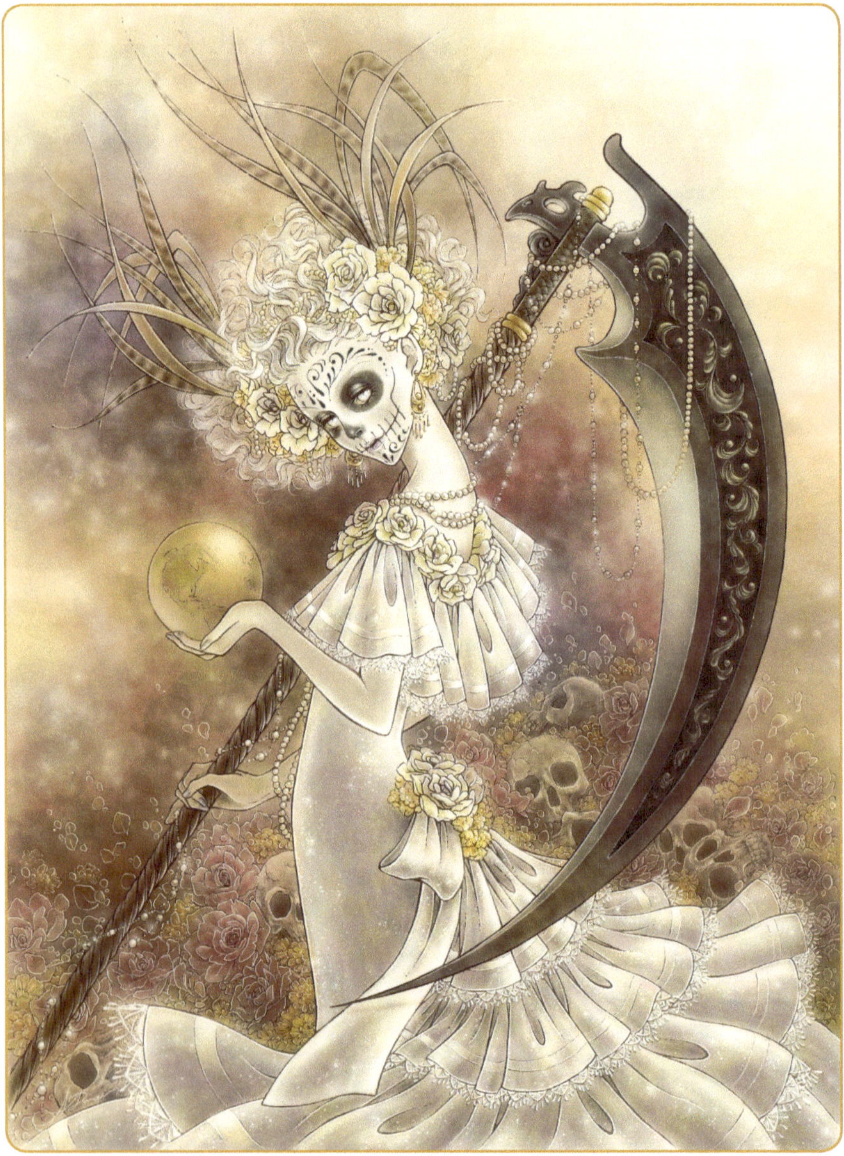

Mitzi Sato-Wluff

CHAPTER 7

Death Of A Friend

Joey's gone from here,
But somewhere now a kitten's born
With Joey's joyous spirit Sing!
Do not mourn.

Winifred Carriere, (1912–2002)

A mouse.
Some yarn.
A moth.
A fly.
But now he's gone:
Kitty,
Goodbye.

Ann Carson, (b. 1929)

I am "Super Cat",
Don't mess with me.
I wear a cape on my back, and a mask,
You see.

Surely I rule,
This house and all here.
Listen carefully, if you want to keep your ear.

Follow my rules,
Don't worry, not many,
I sleep and I eat,
When I am ready.

When I ask for food,
I mean right now.
Not in a minute, and NOT in an hour.

And for heaven's sake,
Don't give me a bath.
Or you will rue the day,
You crossed my path.

Having said all that,
Just one thing more.

Where is my supper?
It's half past four.

By Sheila Delgardo

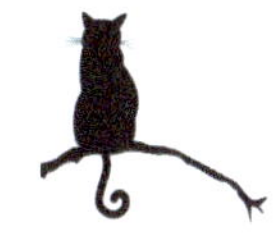

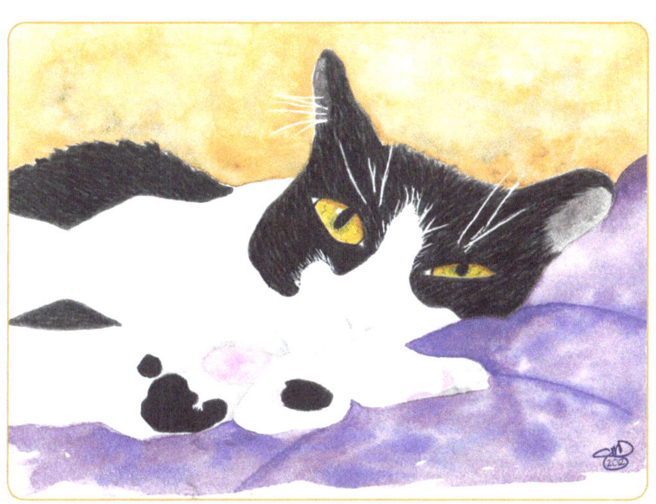

Sheila Delgardo

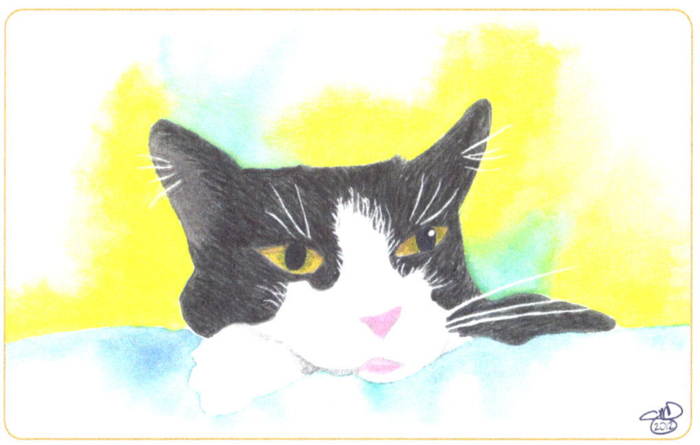

Sheila Delgardo

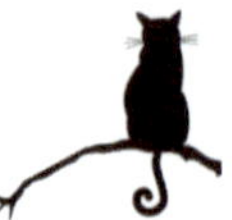

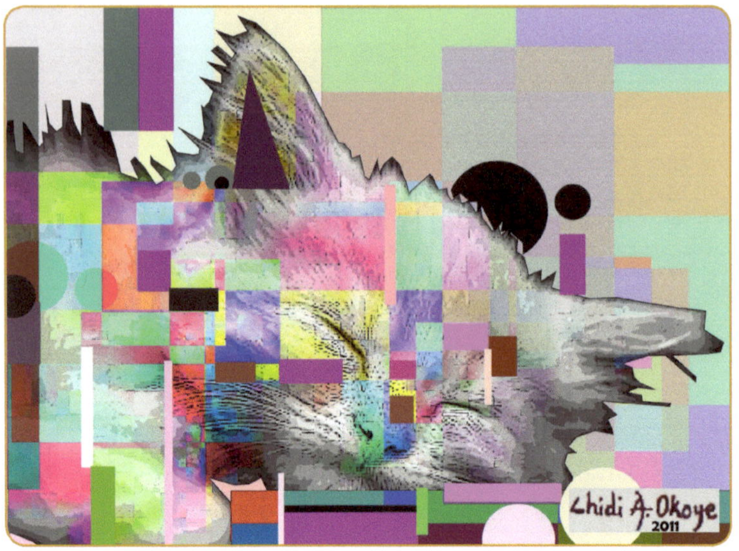

Chidi A. Okoye

A family cat is not replaceable like a worn out coat or a set of tires. Each new kitten becomes its own cat, and none is repeated.

Irving Townsend, (1920–1981)

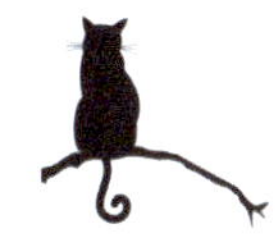

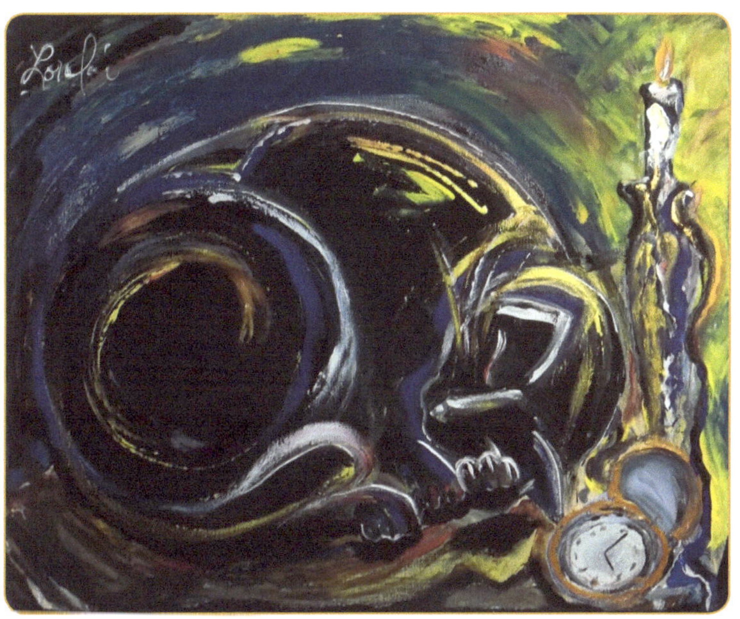

Loralai

Bernice went into a coma and I went out to the backyard to dig a hole. When I got back she was on her feet again, and the whole summer before her death she amused herself by literally jumping in and out of the grave.

Bruce Schimmel, (b. 1956)

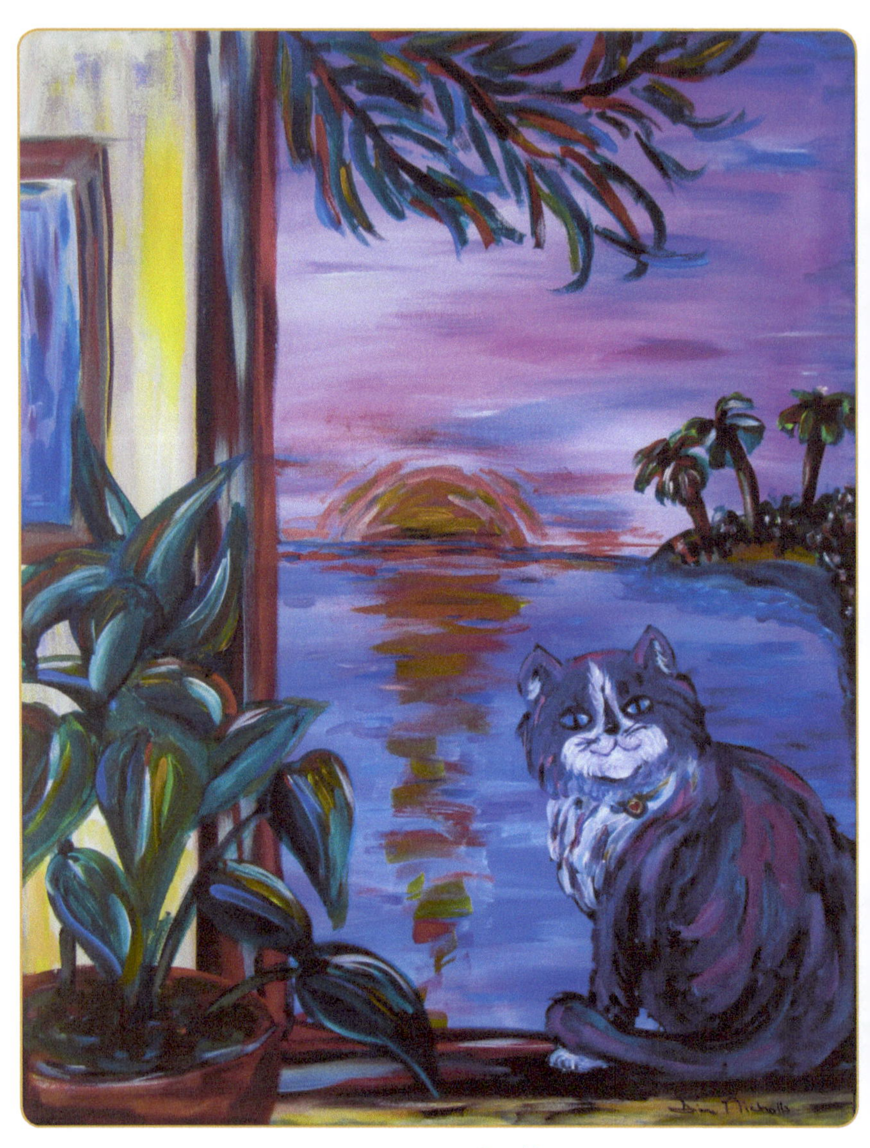

Diane Nicholls

CHAPTER 8

Love Of

The smallest feline is a masterpiece.
Leonardo Da Vinci, (1452–1519)

There are two means of refuge from the miseries of life; music and cats.
Albert Schweitzer, (1875–1965)

A house without a cat, and a well-fed, well-petted, and properly revered cat, may be a perfect house, perhaps, but how can it prove its title?
Mark Twain, (1835–1910)

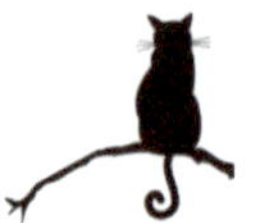

There is not a man living who knows better than I that the four charms of a cat lie in its closed eyes, its long and lovely hair, its silence, and even its affected love.

Hilaire Belloc, (1870–1953)

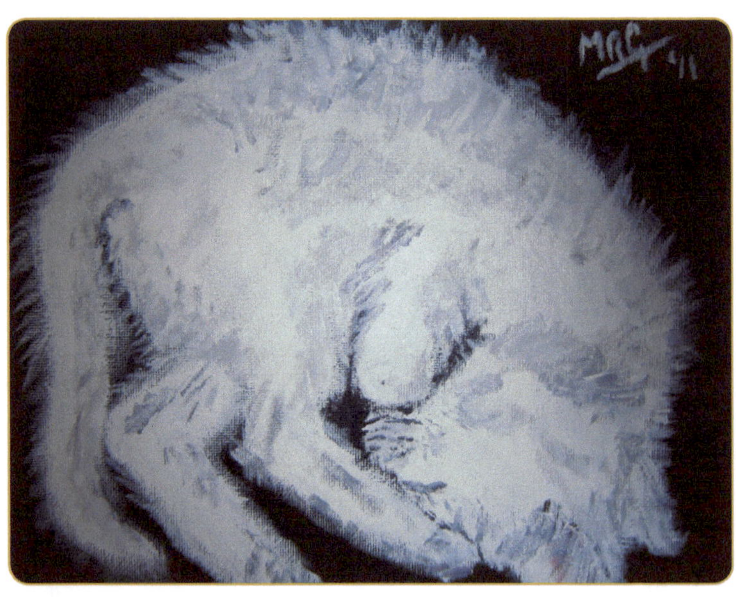

Michael Gardner

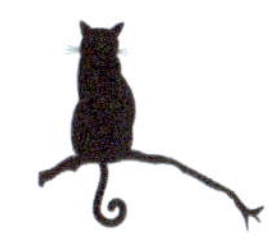

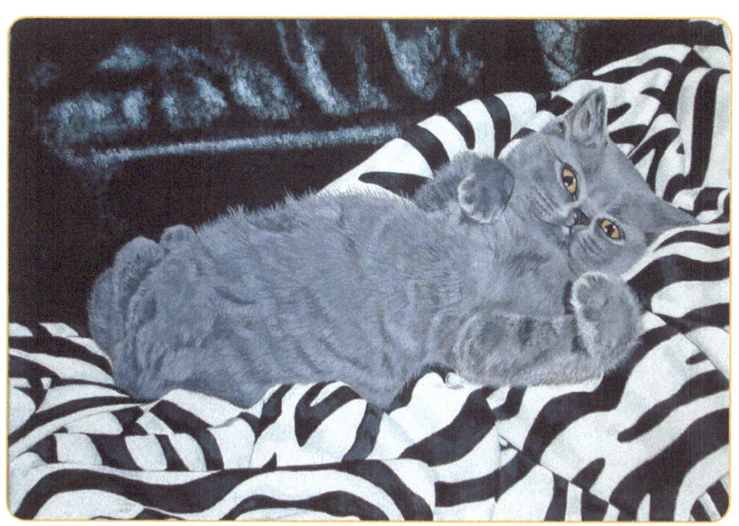

Jennifer Deakin

I respect cats, they seem to have so much else
in their heads besides their mess.
Ralph Waldo Emerson, (1803–1882)

Cats do not declare their love much;
they enact it, by their myriad invocations
of our pleasure.
Vicki Hearne, (1946–2001)

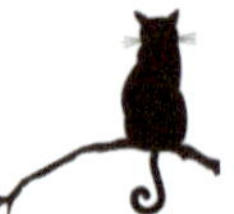

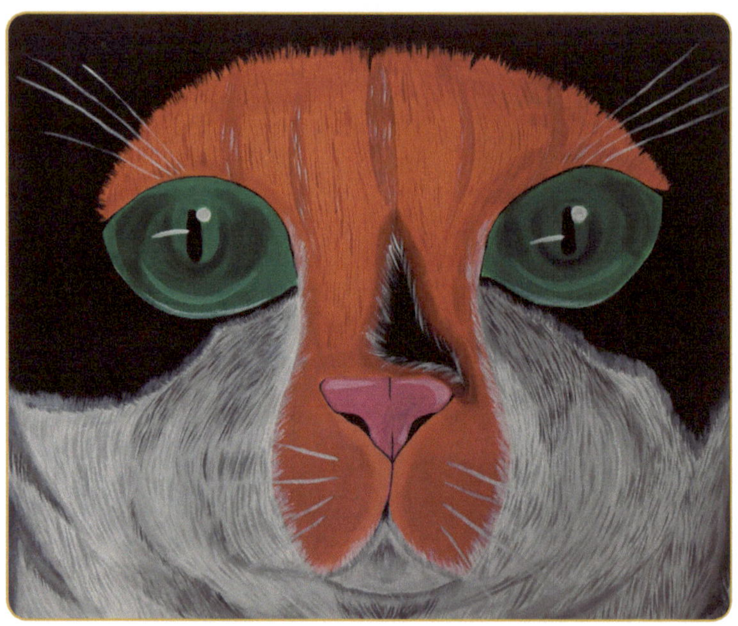

Aubriel Evans

A morning kiss, a discreet tough of his nose
landing somewhere on the middle of my face.
Because his long white whiskers tickled,
I began every day laughing.

Janet F. Faure, (b. 1917)

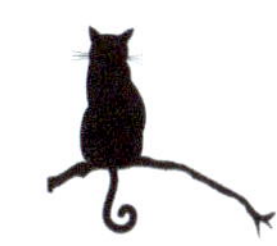

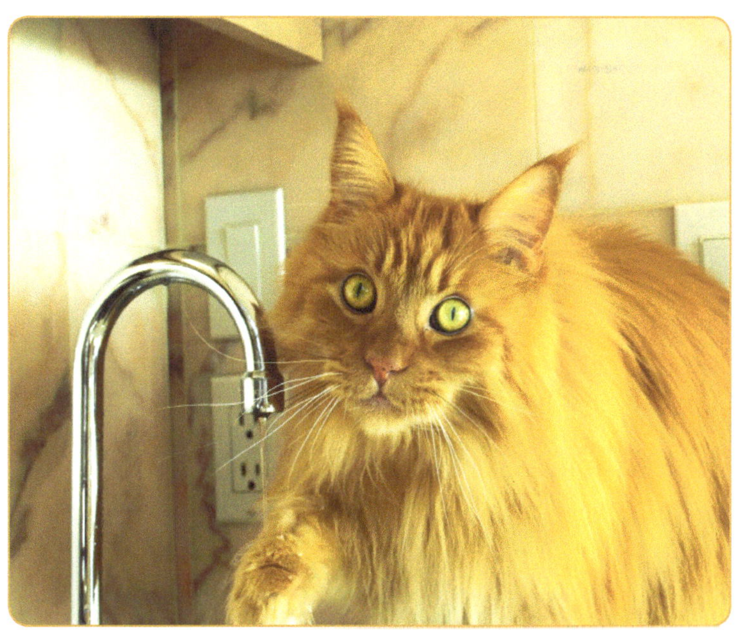

Anait Abramian

I love cats because I enjoy my home; and little by little, they become its visible soul.

Jean Cocteau, (1889–1963)

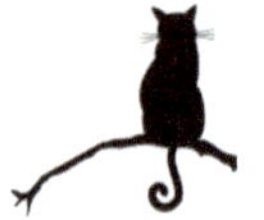

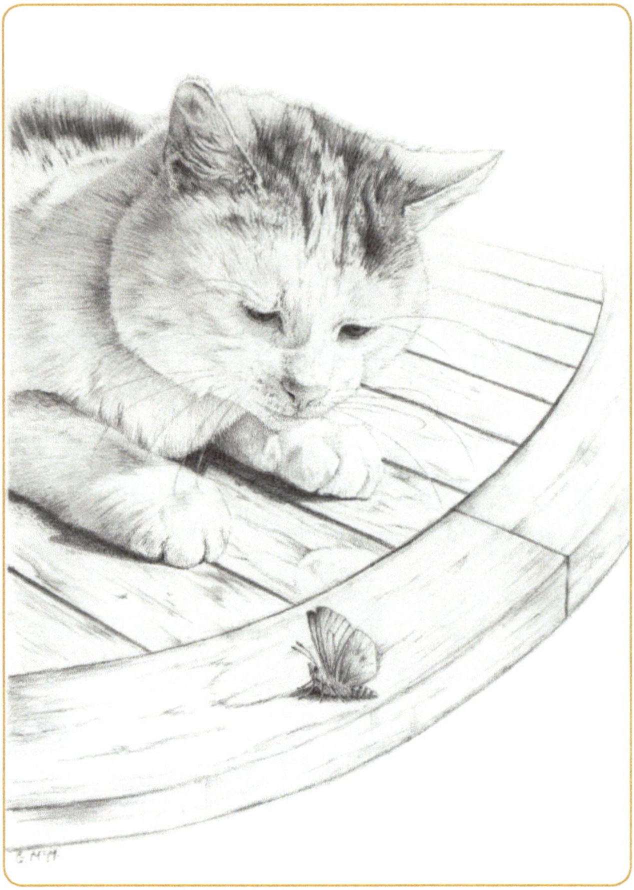

Gillian McMurray

The little furry buggers are just deep, deep wells you throw all your emotions into.

Bruce Schimmel, (b. 1955)

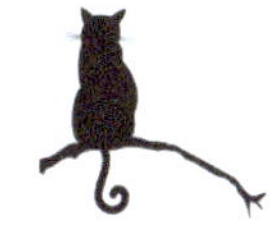

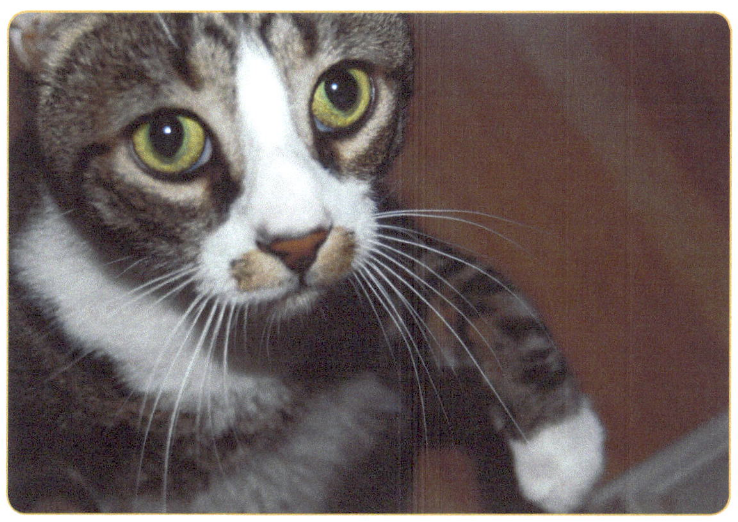

Karen Commings

Slowly, with a look of intense concentration,
he got up and advanced on me. . .put out a
front paw, and stroked my cheek as
I used to stroke his chops.
A human caress from a cat. I felt very meager
and ill-educated that I could not purr.

Sylvia Townsend Warner, (1893–1978)

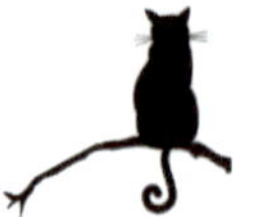

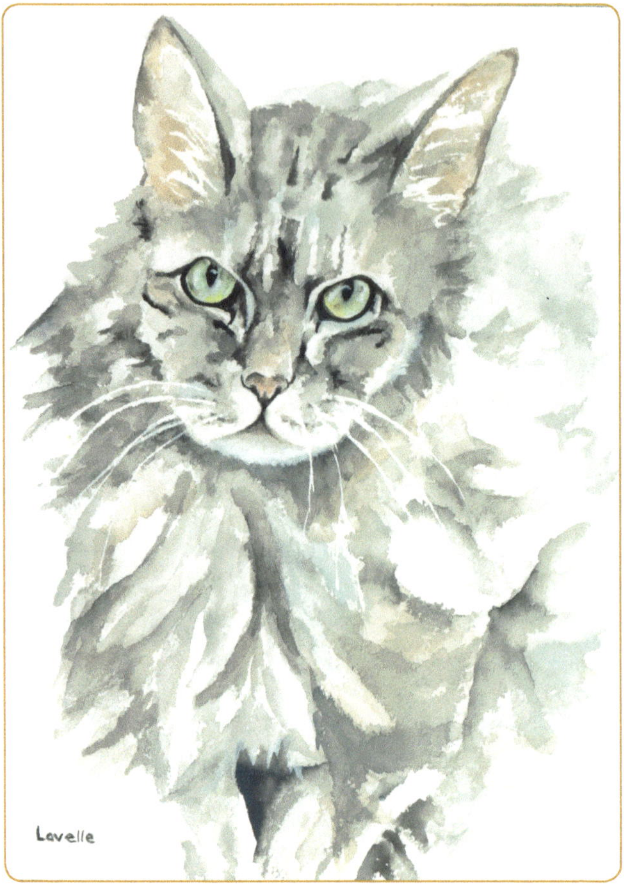

Kimberly Lavelle

One cannot woo a cat after the fashion of the Conqueror. Courtesy, tact, patience, are needed at every step.

Agnes Repplier, (1855–1950)

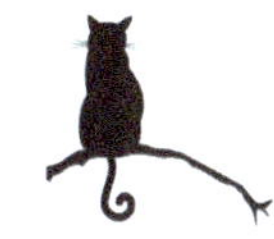

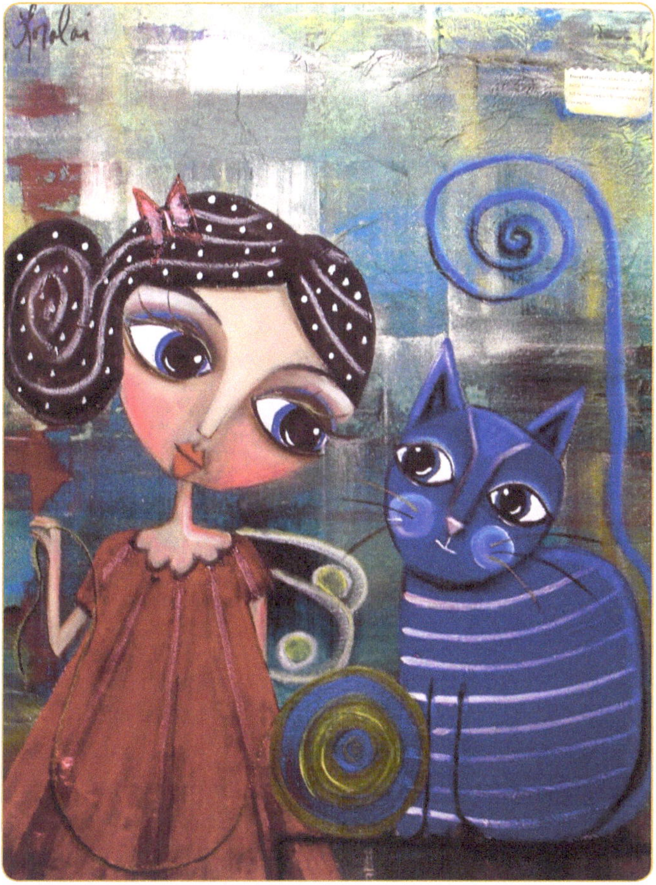

Loralai

Great golden comma of a cat,
You spring to catch my robe's one dangling thread,
And somehow land entangled in my heart.

Lida Broadhurst, (b. 1936)

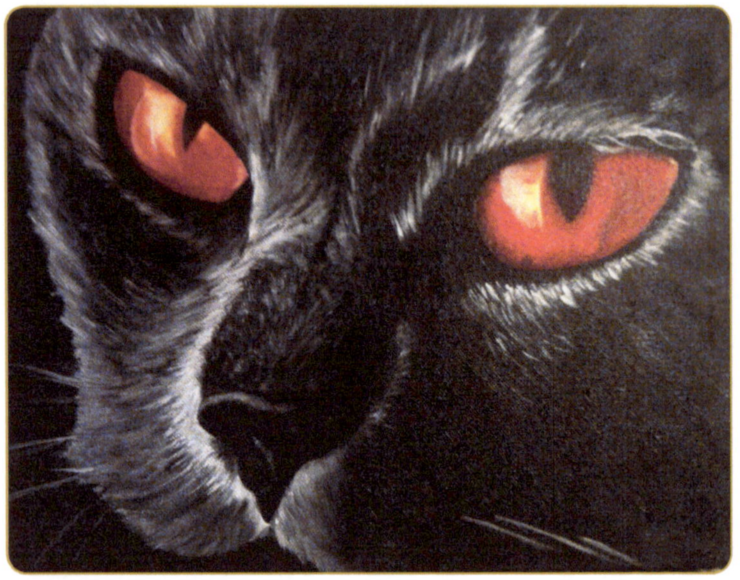

Megan Rawbon

It seems to me that the more useless a cat is the more he has earned his right to companionship. There are enough people "trying to make themselves useful" in this world without the added competition of cats.

Carl Van Vechten, (1880–1964)

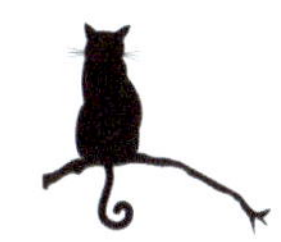

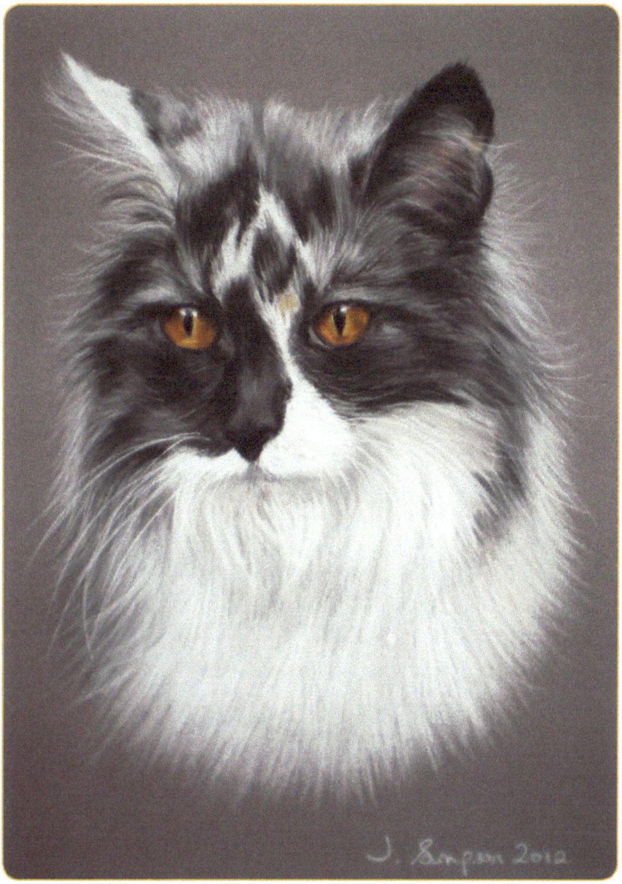

Joanne Simpson-Connor

They're the most graceful, sinuous, sexy, truly sensuous creatures in the world.

Carol Lawrence, (b. 1932)

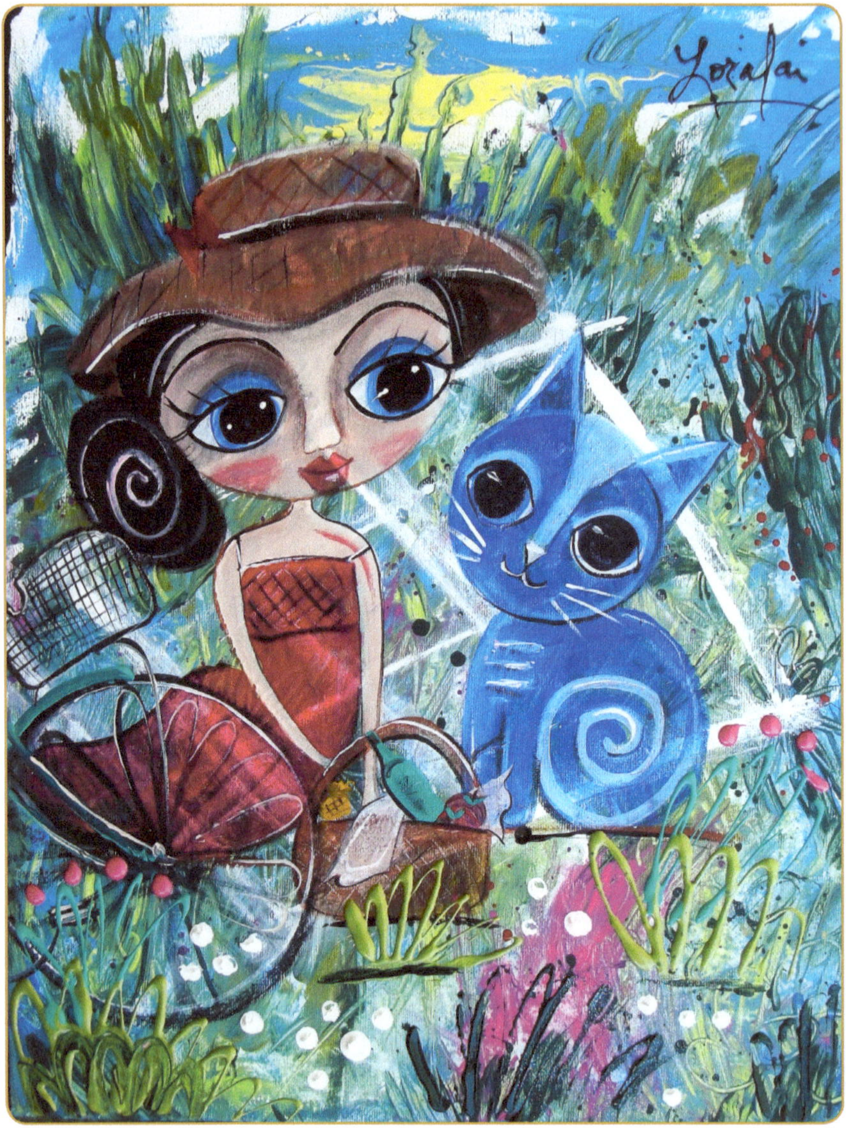

Loralai

CHAPTER 9

Cats Vs. People

To err is human. To purr feline.

Robert Byrne, (b. 1930)

The vanity of man revolts from the serene indifference of the cat.

Agnes Repplier, (1855–1950)

I care not for a man's religion whose dog and cat are not the better for it.

Abraham Lincoln, (1809–1865)

Of all animals, he alone attains the Contemplative Life. He regards the wheel of existence from without, like the Buddha.

Andrew Lang, (1844–1912)

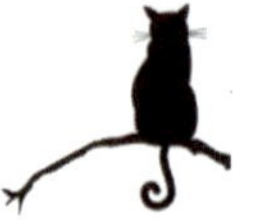

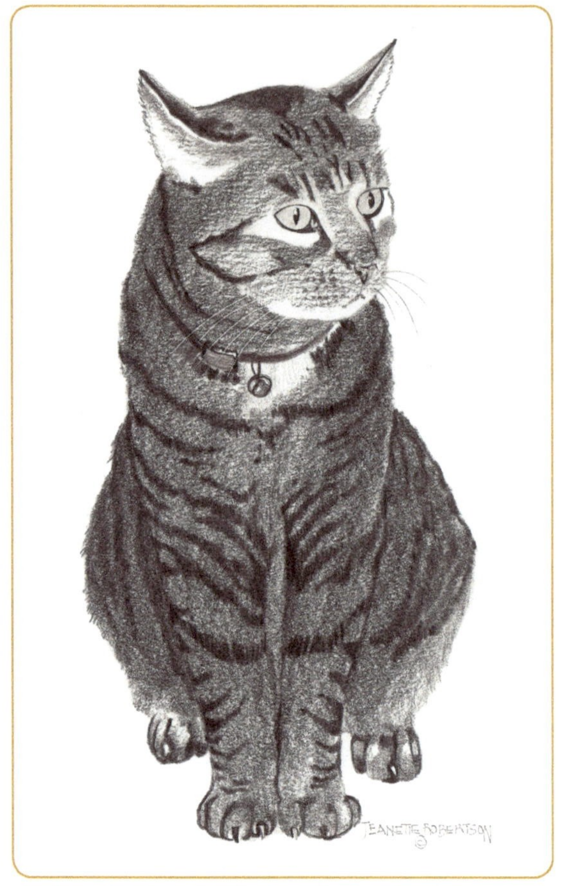

Jeanette Robertson

Only a Frenchman can understand the fine and subtle qualities of the cat.

Theophile Gautier, (1811–1872)

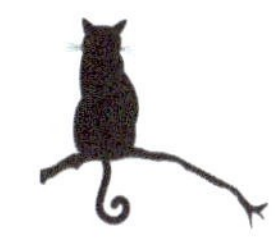

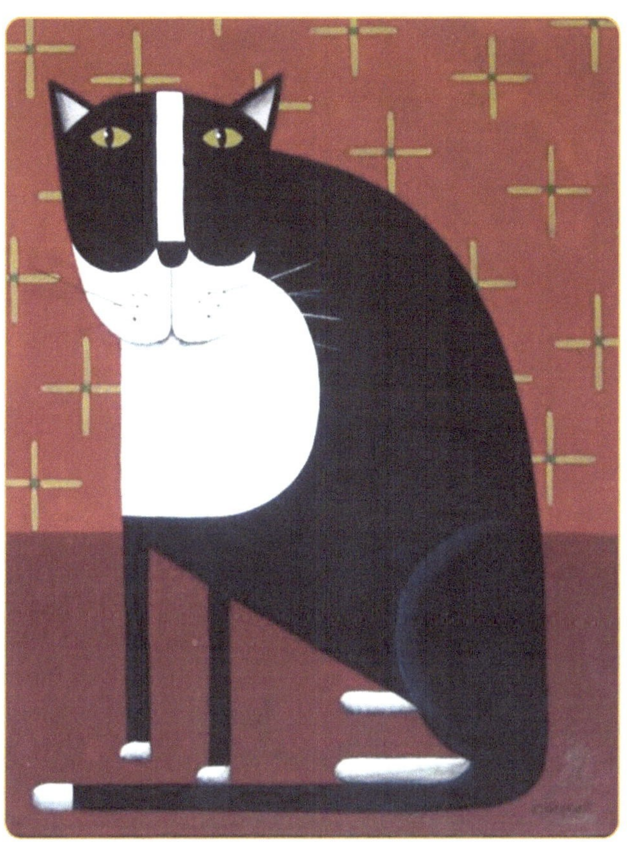

Tim Campbell

In Ancient Egypt they were worshipped as gods. This makes them too prone to set themselves up as critics of the frail and erring human beings whose lot they share.

P. G. Wodehouse, (1881–1975)

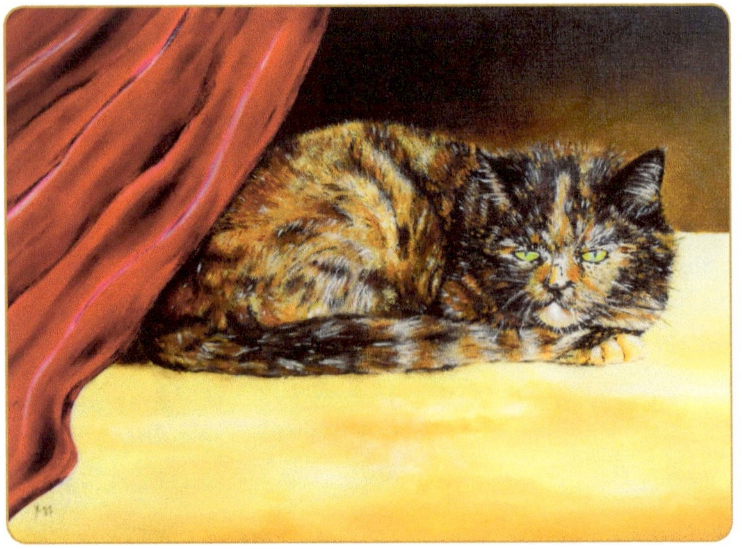

Yvonne Lautenschleager

A cat has absolute emotional honesty:
human beings, for one reason or another,
may hide their feelings, but a cat does not.

Ernest Hemingway, (1899–1963)

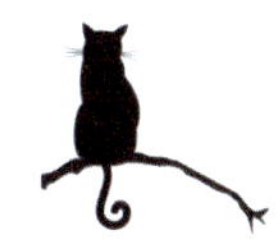

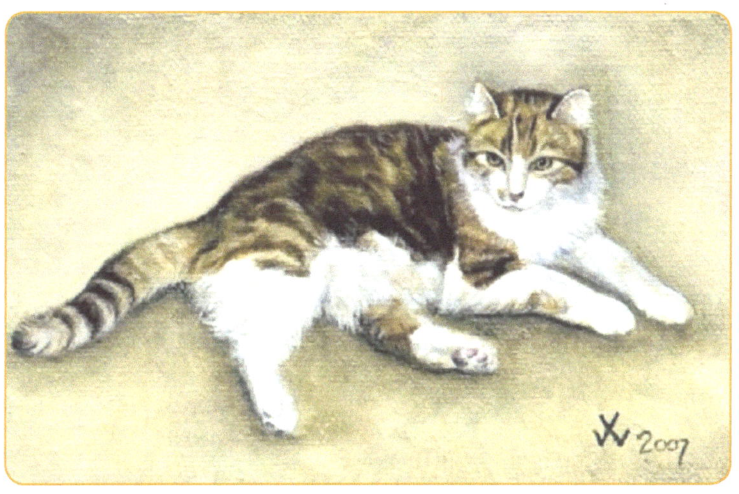

Valarie Wolf

Of all the toys available, none is better designed than the owner himself. A large multipurpose plaything, its parts can be made to move in almost any direction. It comes completely assembled and it makes a sound when you jump on it.

Stephen Baker, (1819–1875)

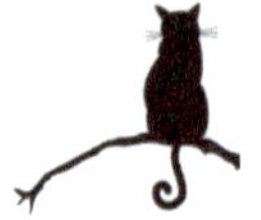

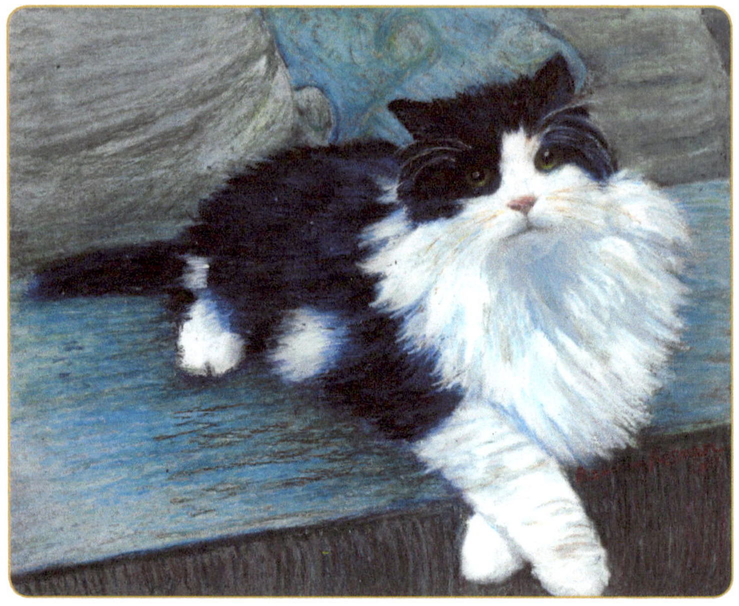

Rebecca Rosman

A cat is never vulgar.
Carl Van Vechten, (1880–1964)

Way down deep, we're all motivated by the same urges. Cats have the courage to live by them.
Jim Davis, (b.1945)

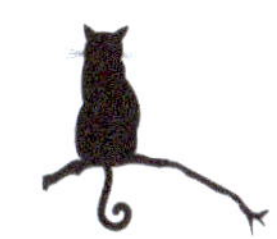

Cats, like women, should be respected as individuals rather than admired as decorations, but there's no harm, given a choice, in taking up with a strikingly attractive specimen of either.

Barbara Holland, (1933–2010)

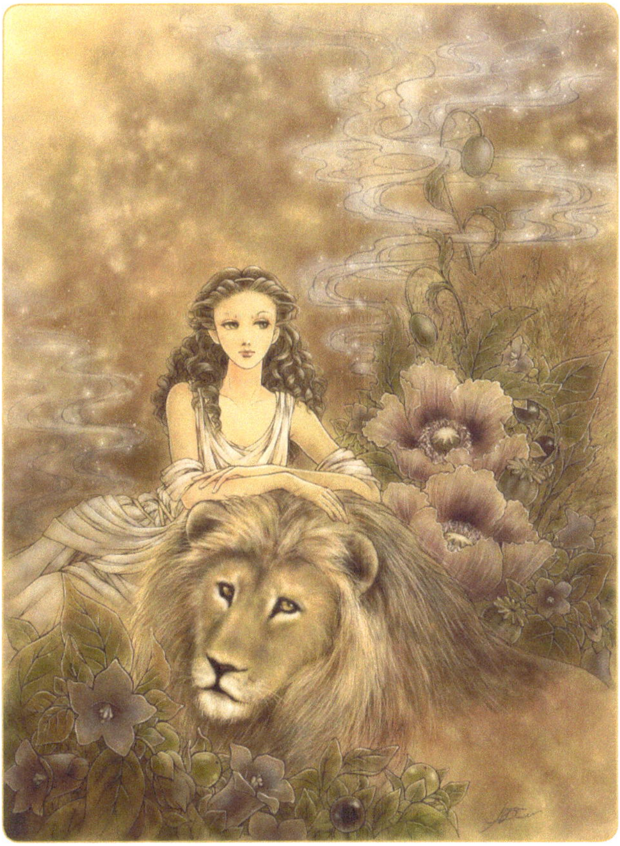

Mitzi Sato-Wluff

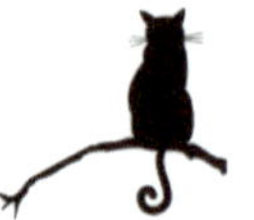

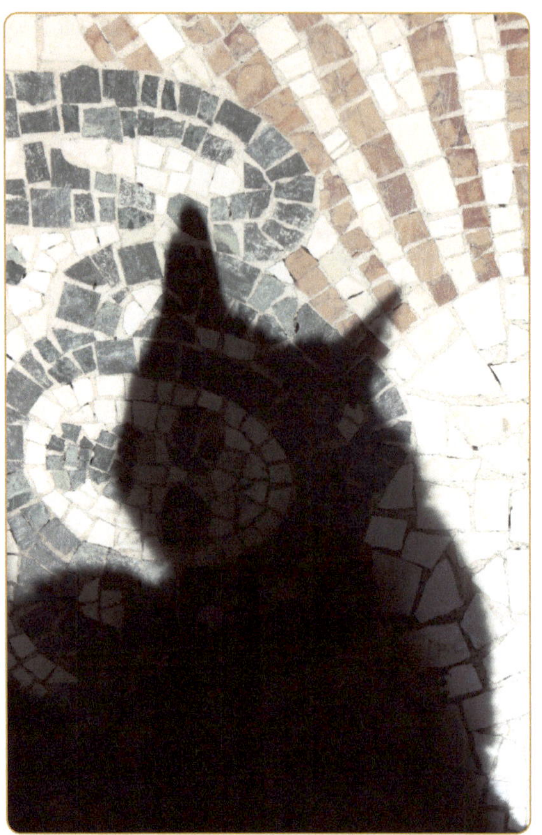

Antonino Falleti

A man has to work so hard so that something of his personality stays alive. A tomcat has it so easy, he has only to spray and his presence is there for years on a rainy day.

Albert Einstein, (1879–1955)

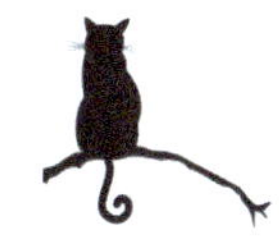

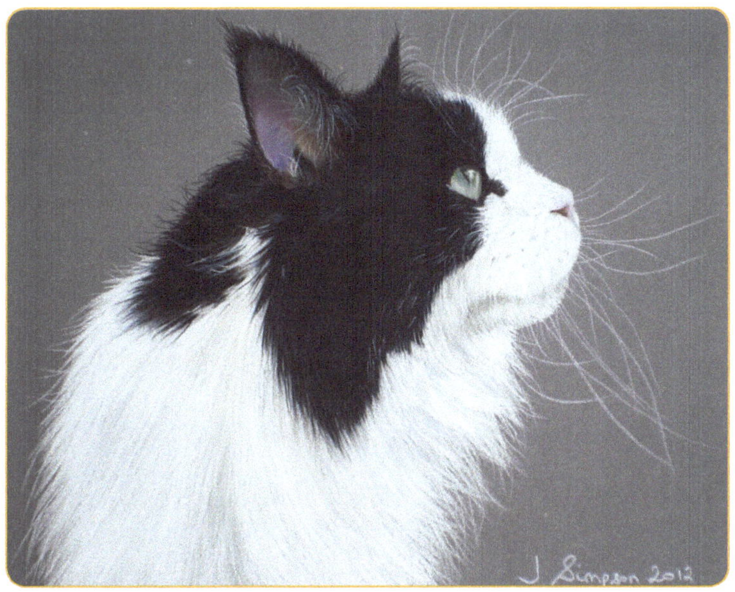

Joanne Simpson-Connor

I think that it is to the cats' credit that neither Hitler nor Napoleon nor Alexander of Macedonia could belong [to cat-loving club]. They feared and hated cats. It is not recorded that a cat ever loved any of the lot, either.

Roger A. Caras, (1928–2001)

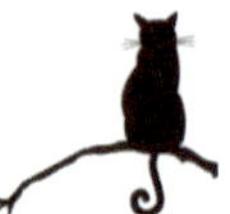

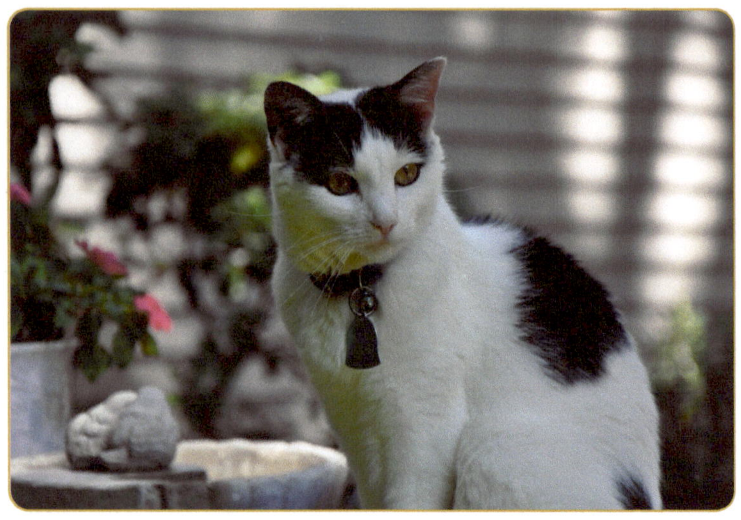

Nancy Howard

I have studied many philosophers and several cats. The wisdom of cats is vastly superior.

Hippolyte Taine, (1818–1893)

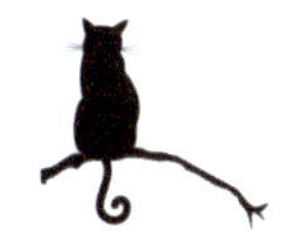

The cat seldom interferes with other people's rights. His intelligence keeps him from doing many of the fool things that complicate life.

Carl Van Vechten, (1880–1964)

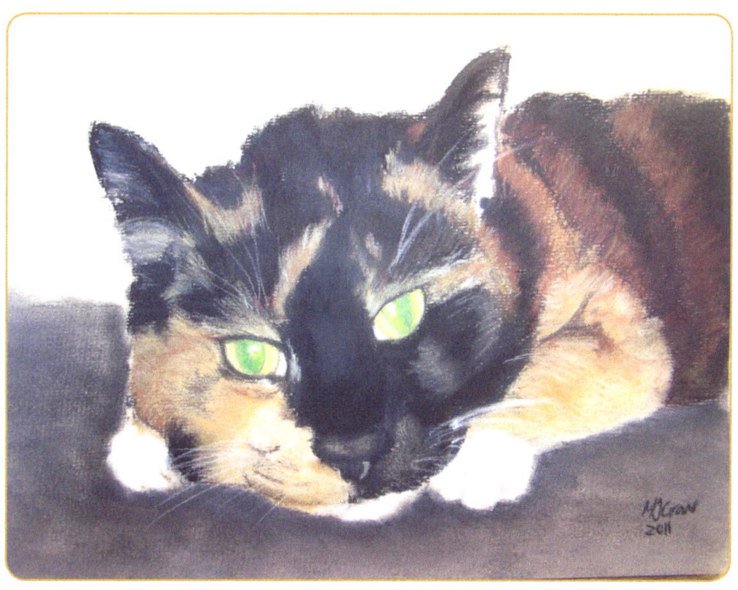

Melissa Crow

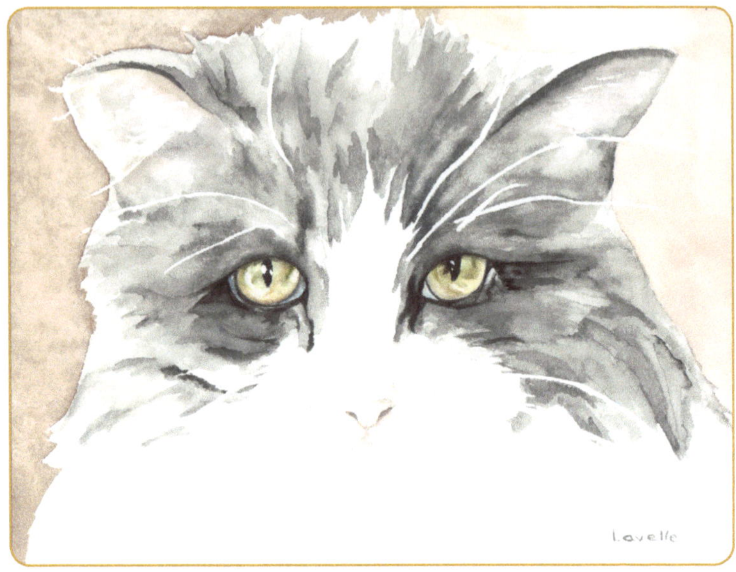

Kimberly Lavelle

A cat can be trusted to purr when she is pleased, which is more than can be said for human beings.

William Ralph (Dean) Inge, (1860–1954)

A god among creatures!
Yet also a stray like me.

Tony Ross, (b.1938)

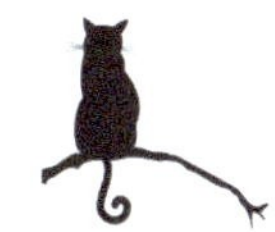

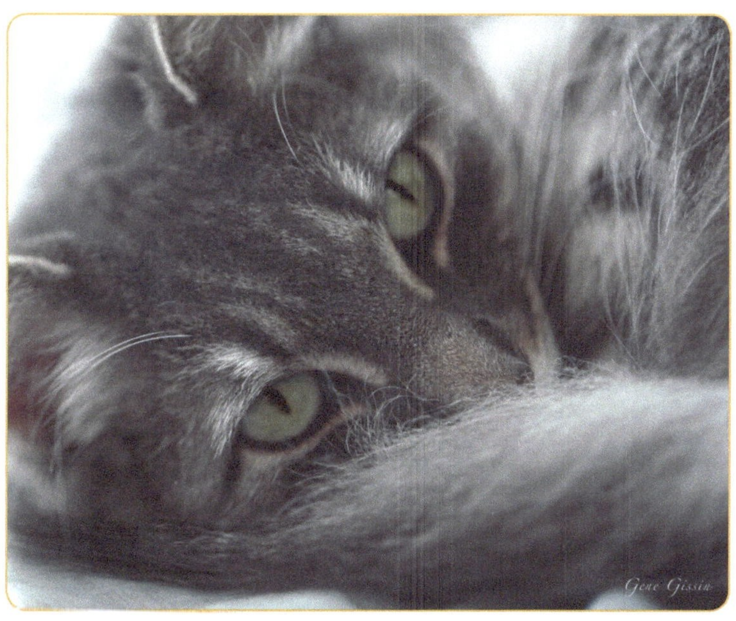

Gene Gissin

We entertain each other with mutual follies, and if I have my time to begin or to refuse, she also has hers.

Michel Montaigne, (1533–1592)

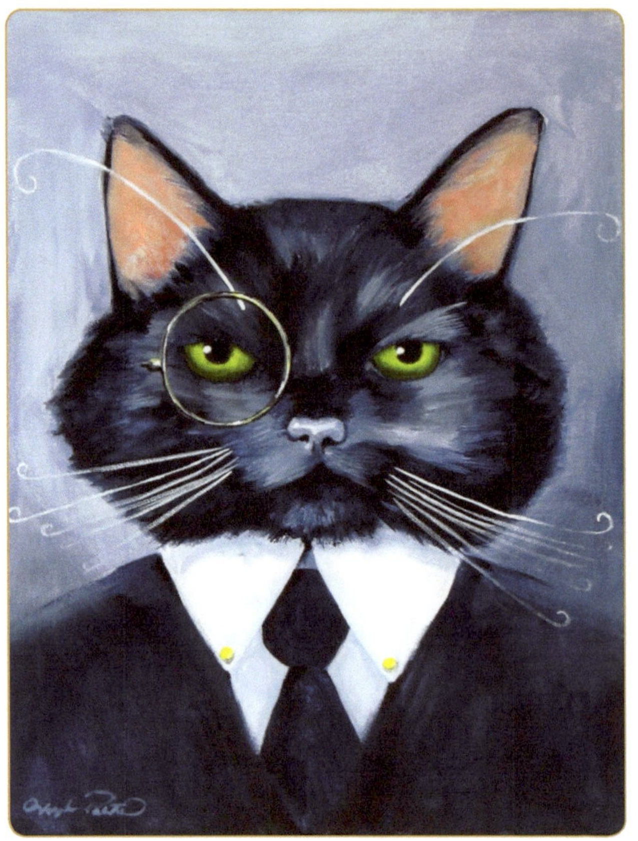

Joseph Palotas

Cats are not people. It's important to stress that, because excessive cat watching often leads to the delusion that cats are people.

Dan Greenburg, (b. 1936)

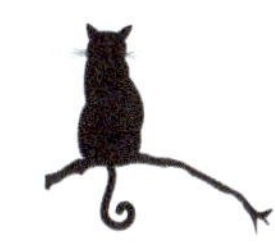

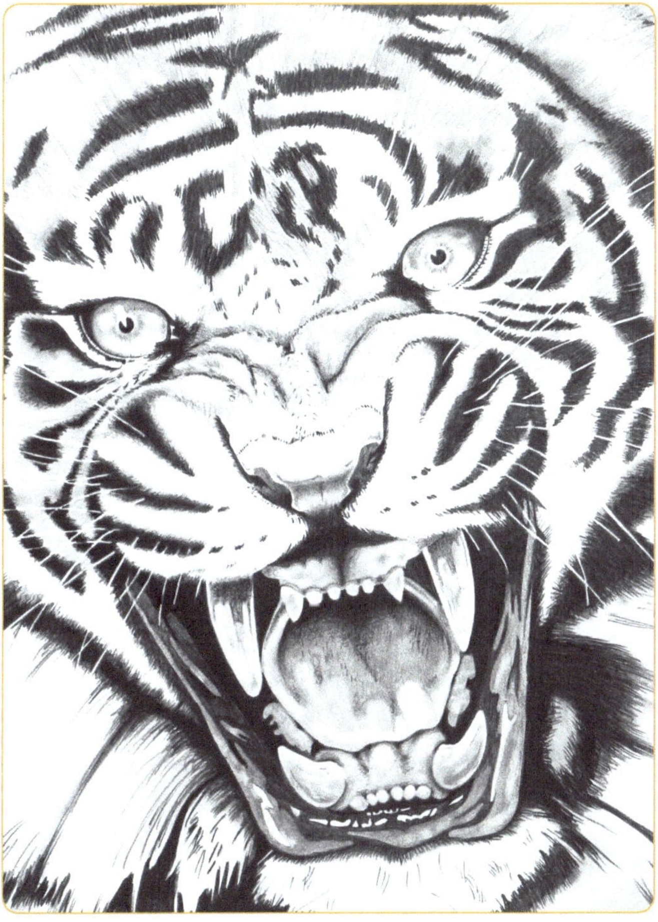

Joseph Palotas

I am the Cat of Cats. I am
The everlasting cat!

William Brighty Rands, (1823–1882)

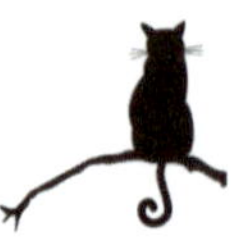

Artists & Photographers Biographies

Anait Abramian—Page 91

A native of Armenia, Anait is a graduate from the Panos Terlemezian College of Fine Arts in Yerevan, Armenia, as well as from the Academy of Art Alexander von Stieglitz in St.Petersburg, Russia. She has exhibited extensively in Eupore and Canada. Anait lives and works in Montreal, where she has been based for many years. You will find her work on facebook under her name and may contact her through facebook or email at modusuper@gmail.com about her work.

Roland Anderson—Page 26, 52

Mr. Anderson is an avid traveler and photographer. A former "Rag Merchant" he now travels extensively throughout Africa, Asia and Europe producing a highly professional photographic collection. Major museums are now vying to produce a major exhibition of his work. He plans no sales of his work until then.

Kayla Ascencio—Page 21, 23, 58,

Kayla was born in a small town located in southwestern Pennsylvania in 1988. She received an Associate in Specialised Business Degree for the illustration program at Douglas Education Center. Kayla's first love is fantasy art. She also enjoys painting animals and portraits. Kayla lives in southwestern Pennsylvania and is currently taking commissions. View her work on her website at www.kaylafantasyart.com or visit her facebook page "Kayla Ascencio Fantasy Art" or on Deviantart www.ascenciok.deviantart.com Contact her at ascenciok@yahoo.com.

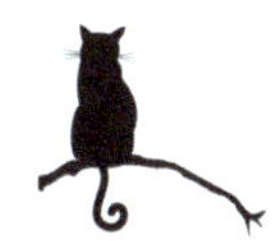

Katrina Avotina—Page 48, 79

Katrina came from Latvia where her family had several generations of artists. She has been exhibiting since the age of 16 and has won several awards. She now lives in the City of Leeds, West Yorkshire, UK. See more of her artwork and contact her on her website and through facebook at www.katrinaavotina.com and www.facebook.com/KatrinaAvotinaPaintings.

Charlotte Blanchard—Page 34

Growing up on a small family farm in Hubbardsville, New York, Charlotte can't remember not drawing or painting. As an only child, she entertained herself for hours on end, escaping into the world of art. At the age of 11, the family made a drastic move to Florida, where Charlotte continued to find solace in the art world. Many of her paintings portray her love for horses and Upstate New York scenery. In 2008, Charlotte became overcome with artistic inspiration when she traveled to Italy for the first time. Her love for Italian architecture, the opulent Mediterranean Sea and the quaint villages came to life on her extraordinary oil canvases. Contact Charlotte at: Wishful Traveler Gallery Hubbardsville, New York 13355 T: 315-691-2265 E: wishfultravelergallery@yahoo.com, www.wishfultravelergallery.com.

Paul Buford—Page 6

Paul Buford is an artist living in Brandon, MS. He was first introduced to watercolor during his studies at the Mississippi State University School of Architecture. Paul is a licensed architect by trade, but has a great passion for art. He finds beauty in the mystery wrapped in decayed, antique, worn items and seeks to explore those hidden stories through many of his works. Paul always welcomes questions regarding commissions, and he can be contacted at breakneckdesigns@gmail.com. You can learn more about Paul from his website www.pebarts.com.

Nathan Bye—Page 22, 27

Nathan is a wildlife and portrait artist from Mansfield, UK. View his artwork at www.paintingsilove.com/artist/nathanbye or on facebook at Nathan Bye—Wildlife and Portrait. Contact him nathanjb@ntlworld.com or nathanjb78@gmail.com.

Tim Campbell—Page 101

Tim describes himself as a self-taught/outsider artist. His work can be seen in galleries throughout New England, Cape Cod, Atlanta and San Francisco. Additionally, his art is featured at the American Folk Art Gallery in New York City. His sculptural pieces are created entirely from recycled wood and metal. His painted furniture uses vintage pieces, which gives them their primitive appearance. Each piece is unique and one-of-a-kind. More information about Tim Campbell's work can be found at www.tcampbellart.com or on his facebook page Tim Campbell Art.

Karen Commings—Page 10, 93

Karen is an artist, photographer, and author. She written seven books about cats, was a columnist and contributing editor for Cat Fancy magazine from 1991-2000, contributing editor for cats at pets.com website, and contributor to Cornell University's Feline Health Center newsleter, CatWatch, from 2000-2005. Her website is www.karencommingsart.blogspot.com. She is also on www.petcareXtra.com and www.paonline.com/commings. Contact her at kcommings@comcast.net.

Melissa Crow—Page 78, 109

Melissa is a self taught artist who was always drawing and painting as a child. Her other passions are running, cats and dogs, and creative writing. She lives with her husband, two daughters, a cat, a dog and tropical fish in Ramsgate, Kent UK. View her artwork on her websites www.animal-

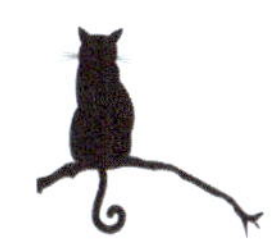

portraitsbymelissa.com and www.melissacrowportraits.com Visit her on facebook page Melissa Crow Animal Portraits. Contact her by email at melissacrow@sky.com.

Jennifer Deakin—Page 21, 89

Jennifer was born in Nottingham UK and took an interest in art from an early age, drawing and painting on almost anything she could find. She discovered she had a talent for painting animals and started to take commissions working from photos. In 2004 Jennifer moved to Spain, living out in the countryside along with her animals, which include dogs, cats and horses. View her work on her websites www.pet-portrait-painting.co.uk and www.myappaloosas.webs.com Visit her facebook page "Jennifer 'Artist' Deakin. People and Pet Portraits". Contact her by telephone or text in Spain 0034 6223813144 and the UK 07767700060.

Sheila Delgardo—Page 83

Sheila studied graphic design and computer graphic arts, but is mainly a self taught artist. She works in watercolor, acrylic, encaustic, pencil, mixed media, digital art, fabric and surface design. She loves animals of all kinds and was blessed to spend 21 years sharing the residence of her gracious and humble cat, Jessie Marie. Sheila writes about health and wellness for Examiner.com.

Contact her at shemar67@gmail.com or on her facebook page. You can see more at the following links.

Spoonflower: www.spoonflower.com/profiles/demouse

They Draw & Cook: www.theydrawandcook.com/search/perform?utf8=%E2%9C%93&keyword=sheila+delgado

They Draw & Travel www.theydrawandtravel.com/maps/historic-san-diego-california-sheila-marie-delgado

Examiner.com: www.examiner.com/wellness-in-santa-ana/sheila-delgado

Andre Dluhos—Page 16, 20, 60

Born 1940 in Slovakia, Andre began to paint at eight years old. At fourteen he won his first art competition from the region's 400 entries. He studied under celebrated artists and mentors at the Bratislava Art School and School of Fine Arts in Uherski Hradiste. Favoring portraiture, figure, and landscape painting, his professional career as a painter began. Traveling and showing throughout Europe, in 1969 he decided to seek new opportunity and a new home in the United States where he now resides. View his artwork at; www.DluhosArts.com, www.DluhosFineArt.com, www.facebook.com/DluhosFineArt, and www.facebook.com/DluhosArts.

Yary Dluhos—Page 28, 62

Born 1944 in Olomouc, Czech Republic. Influenced by the historical and picturesque ambiance of her city, she began to paint in her early childhood. She saw shapes, colors, and textures and only sought to create works that reflected and conveyed the warmth and beauty she observed. She studied at the renown Art School in Uherski Hradiste. Various mediums became a love and her passion earned her numerous rewards in competitive exhibitions. Her creativity and softness of brush lends itself well to various mediums, evidenced throughout the wide range of subject matter she paints. She is a storyteller with her work. View her artwork at; www.DluhosArts.com, www.DluhosFineArt.com, www.facebook.com/DluhosFineArt, and www.facebook.com/DluhosArts.

Aubriel Evans—Page 90

Aubriel is sixteen years old and lives in Ohio. She loves all kinds of art from fantasy to real life. She also enjoys painting objects; She currently paint vases, ornaments and canvasses. Like many artists she loved to draw since she was little. If you wish to see more of her artwork go to her facebook page "*Fantasy Artworks*". To contact Aubriel about her artwork email Aubri_evans@yahoo.com.

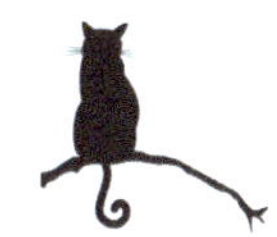

Antonino Falleti—Page 47, 106

Antonino studied etching at People's University, Trieste, decoration in ceramics at The School Decoration, Perugia, and art therapy at The Academy od Fine Arts, Brera, Milan. Visit his blog at antoniofalleti.blogspot.com or on facebook at https://www.facebook.com/antonio.falleti Contact him about his artwork at falleti67@gmail.com.

Dana Feagin—Page 46

Dana has always had a passion for art. After a 20-year corporate career she got serious about oil painting and now is completely focused on animal art—mainly painting pet portraits and shelter/rescue animals that inspire her. Dana generously donates 10% of her art sales back to the Jackson County Animal Shelter and Sanctuary One in Jacksonville, OR. View her artwork at www.inspiredpetportraits.com, www.facebook.com/inspiredpetportraits, www.inspiredpetportraits.etsy.com.

Contact Dana about her work at inspiredpetportraits@yahoo.com.

Lior Immanuel Fischer—Page 59

Lior was born in Bern Switzerland and developed an interest in art at an early age. He enjoys producing artwork that explores the psychological effect colors can have on the human mind and mood. See more of Lion's work at www.modernartist.webs.com or visit him on facebook at www.facebook.com/modernartlf.

Quinne Fokes—Page 9, 73

Quinne Fokes, who is an Augusta, Georgia native, now lives in San Anselmo, CA, and studied art at Sweet Briar College, Virginia, UNC Greensboro, and earned an MFA in visual arts from the Maryland Institute's Mt. Royal School. The portraits you see today are just one area of her artwork, which you'll find at www.quinne.com. She paints expressive impressions of animals, and welcomes commission requests for cats, dogs, horses with their people. Her studio manager is Cachilla Ruth, the fine cat. View her work on her website www.quinnedesign.com. Contact her by email at q@quinnedesign.com.

Michael Gardner—Page 88

Michael is a UK based painter. His approach to his artwork is "Put some paint, glue, various stuff and a lot of love onto a canvas, arrange it into something I like, show it to other people to see if they like it, invite comments". View his work on his facebook page "Michael Gardner (Mr.G) Painter" Contact him at mg2993pinlibrary@yahoo.co.uk.

Clara Milleret Germanotta—Page 66

Clara is a young artist from Paris, France. She is also an accomplished guitarist. View her works on these websites www.facebook.com/LittleMonsterCla... , twitter.com/LilMonsterClara, www.youtube.com/user/ByCl4r4xD.

Gene Gissin—Page 65, 111

Gene Gissin is a graduate of RIT College of Graphic Arts and Photography. He owns Gene Gissin Photography where he specializes in photographing everything from weddings to pets. Further, Gissin also works in photojournalism and has taught photography at Cazenovia College in Cazenovia, New York. Today, he is the President of the Professional Photographers Society of Central New York. For more of Gissin's work, visit his website at www.gissinphoto.com.

Claudia Hahn—Page 25, 77

Claudia is working as a freelance graphic designer and wildlife artist based in Surrey, southern England. Growing up in the beauty of the Black Forest, Germany, she developed her love of nature from a very early age. Claudia studied

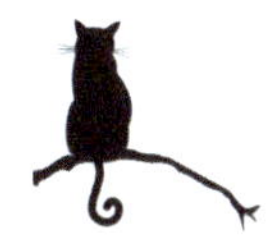

graphic design in Freiburg, Germany, and later specialised in book illustration and wildlife art. She is exhibiting her work in galleries all over Europe and the USA, and has sold original artworks to private art collectors in Germany, Switzerland, Denmark, France, England, Israel and the USA. She has been around the globe on assignments, commissions, missions, exhibitions and sometimes just plain stalking amazing wildlife for new artwork. View her work at www.heliocyan.com and www.bosmansandhahn.com.

Traci Hallstrom—Page 51

Traci found her love for ceramic mosaic art almost by accident when she enrolled in a class she thought was on stain glass are and was in fact a ceramics class. She never looked back. You view her at the following locations: www.fluffypuppiesmosaics.com, www.flickr.com/photos/fluffypuppiesmosaics, www.fluffypuppiesmosaics.wordpress.com and www.twitter.com/mosaicstones. On her facebook page "Fluffy Puppies Mosaics Art" Contact Traci at Traci.Hallstrom@gmail.com or by phone at 530-339-0210.

Nancy Howard—Page 69, 108

Nancy is a cat lover and amateur photographer. She lives in Fairfield Conn. and is an Academic Coach and Psychology Tutor at Fairfield University. Even with a BS from Cornell University and a PHD from University of Rochester in Psychology she is often unable to decipher the thoughts of her cat Kashmire.

Susan Kordish—Page 38, 67

Susan has been a photographer for a number of years. She has done freelance work for "The Horse", and "Trail Blazer" magazine. She has had work appear in Yankee Pedlar and a Canadian Team Penning magazine. She is a member of the Association of Photoshop Professionals and the Professional Photographers Association. She has taken some college level classes, online classes and just attended an amazing Photoshop seminar. Susan has recently begun entering photography contest and some juried art shows. She also makes and sells photo note cards. Visit her website www.azcowgirlphotography.com her facebook page Cowgirl Photography or contact her at Susan Kordish PO Box 204 Skull Valley, Arizona 86338 cowgirlphotography@hughes.net.

Katerine Koukiotis (aka katerinaart)—Page 32, 36

Katerina is a professional fantasy/portraiture traditional artist from N.Y. Her style of art is realism, she specialises in pencil hand drawn portraits and fantasy paintings. Katerina loves drawing and painting, fairy tales, mythology, Animals, Gothic, Mermaids, Angels, Inspirational, and anything that inspires her. Katerina has won several art contests, her art is published in books and has done numerous commissions for clients. To view her artwork or contact her about commissions or purchases visit her website http://www.katerinaart.com.

Yvonne Lautenschlaeger (aka medea)—Page 102

Yvonne is a Hamburg, Germany based artist. She has a medical degree and has worked in Orthopedic Medicine as well as Chinese Medicine. She is married with a twenty-year-old son, a dog and two cats. She is working as a full time painter since 2009 and very active creating new art, writing and maintaining her blog. To see more of Yvonne's work, visit http://www.medeasspace.de.

Kimberly Lavelle—Page 94, 110

Kimberly is an award winning artist who has been exposed to fine art since childhood. She studied art at St. Edwards University in Austin, Texas. The majority of her work has been commissioned animal portraits and raptor paintings. Her intent with all of her portrait work is to capture

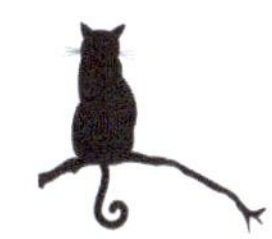

and honor each individual personality and shows the spirit that she sees shining out through their eyes. Kimberly works with the Fort Collins Cat Rescue and Rocky Mountain Raptor Program donating works for their annual fund raisers and donating 25% of all commissioned work associated with their organizations back to them. View her work and contact her at www.fromtheheartwatercolors.com and http://fineartamerica.com/profiles/kimberly-lavelle.html.

Grace Lipker—Page 33

Grace is a photographer who specializes in animal portraits. View her work on her facebook page "Grace Lipker Animal Portraits" or contact her at imfloatingaway3@aim.com.

Loralai (Loryia Bond)—Page 85, 95, 98

Loralai lives in Columbus Ohio and is a life long art lover. Her Blue Cat Series is inspired by a rescue cat named Blue. Loralai is actively involved in promoting foster care and adoption of cats in need. She regularly donates a portion of the proceeds from her art sales to these worthy causes. See more of her artwork at: www.facebook.com/loralaioriginalart, www.etsy.com/shop/mermaidartbyloralai, www.fairyartbyloralai.blogspot.com.

Contact her about her artwork at; admin@loralai.com, loryia.bond@gmail.com, and by phone at; 614-5610-344.

Milena Matic—Page 53

Milena was born and raised in Chicago. She now lives in the Pacific Northwest. Her work is displayed throughout Portland and has reached customers throughout the United States. Her paintings are on display in restaurants and cafes from Portland to Bend, Oregon. Her work has been in gallery shows on the coast and the L.A. Underground Art Show in Portland. Each year she participates in the Gresham Art Walk. You can view Milena's work on her website at www.

mojiexpressions.com or follow her on Facebook and Twitter. Her work has been described as "having a Picasso touch with an urban feel."

Anne Redmond McFarland—Page 30, 42

Anne is an artist, photographer, and cat lover. Given her career demands she is currently unable to spend as much time on her artwork as she would like.

Gillian McMurry—Page 71, 92

Gillian has been painting and drawing since childhood and has over 20 years experience working with watercolor and graphite. She specializes in painting and drawing animals, both wild and domestic, and architecture in both media as well as colored pencil and pen and ink. Her passion for painting and drawing is only surpassed by her love of animals, especially the local wildlife. A more than willing participant in wildlife conservation, she can frequently be found prowling the Scottish countryside in search of local wildlife to inspire her. More information about Gillian and her work can be found at http://gillianmcmurray.webs.com.

Sue McNulty—Page 49

Sue has two major loves in her life, animals and my paintings. She has been a professional artist for the last 25 years. Her love for both started when she was a child. View her artwork on her facebook page Sue's Pet Art or on the web at; www.thedogliberator.com, www.suespetart.blogspot.com, www.art-cafe.net/?p=52, www.SuesPetArt.esty.com.

Jeff Montagne—Page 56

Jeff is a wildlife artist from Sacrameto, CA. He has been featuring wildlife in his artwork for over 10 years and has won numerous art awards. His deep respect for wildlife helps create his passion for his work. View his artwork on his face-

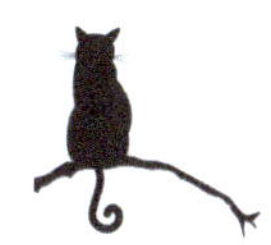

book page "Wildlife Art by Jeff Montagne" or at; www.twitter.com/@WildlifeArtbyJM, www.renaissancehouse.net, and www.rawartists.org/wildlifeartbyjm.

Contact him at wildlifeartbyjm@yahoo.com.

Jessica Morgan-Chase—Page 68

Working mostly in graphite, Olympia artist Jessica Morgan-Chase strives to capture the unique expressions, thoughts and feelings of animals and mythical creatures through her art. She intends to provoke feelings of peace, but also power as seen and felt in our natural world. Jessica works out of her home studio located in Olympia, Washington. You can contact her and view her art on her website www.jessicachaseart.com or on her facebook Page: www.facebook.com/pages/The-Art-of-Jessica-Morgan-Chase/132999786744009?v=info.

Diane Nicholls—Page 50, 76, 86

Diane likes fun and color in her paintings. Messages and/or hidden meanings are common in her work, but some paintings are just for fun. Absence of detail is an objective she uses in her style of painting. Abstract Realism and/or Fauvism closely describes her style, although her own personal style is unique. Being an avid Christian, she often uses this in her work. Born in a suburb of Pittsburgh, she attended college in Ohio, raised 3 beautiful children and is now starting a new adventure in the Houston area. Diane is a member of the Conroe Art League in Texas. Visit her shop on Etsy: http://www.etsy.com/shop/dianenicholls.

Childi A. Okoye—Page 45, 84

Childi born in Nigeria graduated with a distinction in sculpture (Higher National Diploma) from the Institute of Management and Technology in Enugu, Nigeria, in 1988. For the next six years he taught sculpture and drawing at

Federal Polytechnic Oko Anambra State Nigeria. In Nigeria, He had his national solo exhibition "Textures of Life" and launching of his book "Lamentation" at national museum Lagos in 1993 sponsored by Mobil Producing Nigeria. Okoye is as famous for his poetry as for his painting and sculpture. In 1994 Okoye moved to Vancouver, Canada. View his work at; www.modernartimages.com contact his at 604 628 7402.

Kristin Palmer—Page 37

Kristin was born on April 9th in the small state of Rhode Island, where she still currently resides. Kristin has been drawing and creating art since she could hold a pencil. Working almost entirely in watercolor she specialises in creating the haunting and mysterious world of the Fae. As a budding artist Kristin is enthusiastically launching herself into a career as a professional artist. Kristin works at keeping her art fresh and new, and is always open to new and exciting artistic opportunities. Visit her website www.mysticfaefantasart.weebly.com on her facebook page Mystic-Fae-Fantasy-Art Email: mysticfaeart@aol.com Twitter:@MysticFaeArt.

Joseph Palotas—Page 112, 113

Joe is an experienced commission artist and works in many media. He infuses wild expressions of color to a wide variety of subject matter from portraits, to abstracts to contemporary and mixed media landscapes. His works reflect a variety of creative styles. See more of Joe's work at his facebook page Art In Wonderland or on his websites, http://www.artsinwonderland.com.

Ema Paraschiv—Page 44

Ema is a professional artists from Bucuresti, Romania. Her work has won numerous awards and international competitions. View her artwork on her website of on facebook at;

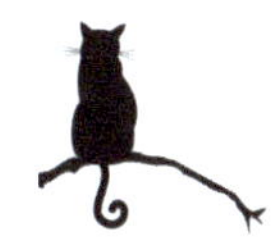

www.emaparaschiv.tk, www.facebook.com/emaparaschivart. Tel: 07289 7777 2.

Penny Price—Page 35, 40

Penny is an Australian Painter who has combined her love of all creatures great & small with her passion for painting to offer unique, modern, vibrant Pet Portraits & Customized artworks from her website Pet Brush Art. Penny is qualified in the traditional art of hand painted sign wrting and is currently studying a certificate in Companion Animal services. Penny donates from her artwork to animal welfare and can be contacted through her website www.petbrushart.com or facebook page Pet Brush Art.

Magan Rawbon—Page 96

Magan is a degree student from Derbyshire, UK. She has always enjoyed art in a variety of ways but has recently found a real passion for painting. She works with oil paint as she loves the textures and flexibility it allows. Magan mainly paint realistic portrayals of animals. View her work at www.facebook.com/WaltonAnimalPortraits.

Garrett Redmond—Page 19, 24

Garrett has a wide range of interests photography and a love of cats are just two of them.

Jeanette Robertson—Page 100

Jeanette is an artist and published author of art books [see them on amazon.com]. She works in watercolor and graphite pencil. Jeanette specializes in pet drawings but does much more. You can find her art on: www.CottageArtStudio.Etsy.com or www.jeanetterobertson.com. Contact her at jrobertsonart@aol.com.

Rebecca Rosman—Page 8, 74, 104

Rebecca is a Landscape Designer and Artist based in Seattle. She specializes in painting animal portraits, using oil pastels. Why paint cats? Because they are complex and lovely. Why paint dogs? Because they are such happy souls. With a bachelor's degree in Landscape Architecture (University of Washington), Rebecca has been drawing and designing for the last fifteen years. She has shown her artwork in juried art shows, art walks and coffee shops in Seattle and has commissioned pet portraits nationally. She can be reached at rebecca@modernpetart.com. View her work at; www.facebook.com/modernpetart and www.modernpetart.com.

Linda Rufo—Page 57, 61

Linda has BFA from the University of the Philippines. She is a professional freelance artist now working in New York, NY. She has won numerous awards for her artwork. View her work and contact her through her facebook page "Linda Rufo Art."

Mitzi Sato-Wluff—Page 75, 80, 105

Mitzi is a relative newcomer to the world of fantasy art, although she has been making art for a long time. Her distinct images are created by combining traditionally rendered line art in pen on paper with her unique digital coloring technique, using Corel Painter program, resulting in a look similar to works done in watercolor. When she's not painting fantasy images, she enjoys teaching Japanese to American students, playing the piano, taking care of her goldfish and freshwater tropical fish tanks, playing with her family cats, gardening, cooking, and reading." View her work at; www.auroawings.com or on her facebook page "Fantasy Art of Mitzi" Contact her at studiomiyabi@aol.com.

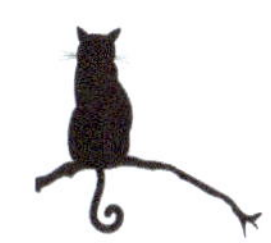

Patricia Elliott Seitz—Page 14

Patricia was born in San Diego California, and spent most of her young adulthood living in Southern California. She came from a background of art and music, and always knew that she wanted to be an artist. Her love for landscapes and seascapes has been heavily influenced by where she has lived through the years. Her painting approach is based on Impressionism, and Tonalism. Her main subject matter is landscapes, and seascapes. Today she can be found in her studio, painting seasonal paintings of the Central New York area, and the California coastlines. She is an active member of Oil Painters of America, CNY Art Guild, and her work is represented by Local NY art Galleries. See more of her work at www.patriciaseitz.com.

Joanne Simpson-Connor—Page 97, 107

Joanne is an award winning professional pastel pet portrait living in High Peak Derbyshire, UK. She works from photographs to produce a true likeness of pets, using only the highest quality pastels and paper. View her artwork and follow her blog on these websites; www.joannes-petportraits.co.uk, www.zazzle.co.uk/jopetportraits, www.jo-petportraits.blogspot.com, and www.groovycart.co.uk/uniquecards.co.uk.

Angela Skea—Page 18, 27

Angela Skea is a self-taught artist from South Africa. With a background in Nature Conservation, Angela has a passion for African wildlife from which she gets her inspiration. Angela's preferred medium is water colors, she also enjoys experimenting with new mediums and techniques and has enjoyed a love for art since her childhood. View her works on her facebook page; "Angela Skea Wildlife Art" or contact her at skeastudio@gmail.com and +2782 922 7071.

Cal Slater—Page 31, 43

Cal is from the United States. He has been doing art and animation for years, but just recently began painting animal portraits. He uses Adobe Flash, Photoshop, and Corel Painter to create the art. To commission him, visit his website www.stringstudiopro.com or his facebook page "String Studio Productions LLC" or send an email to ctslater@yahoo.com.

Sue Spina—Page 12

Sue is a cat lover and photographer. Her Maine Coon Cat Oscar is most engaging and a source of constant pleasure.

Samantha Thompson—Page 11

Samantha's pastel and acrylic paintings display a complex of influences from her rich and varied life. She was born in Sydney in 1978. Having worked and exhibited around the world including New York and London, her last major influence was living in the most 'art deco' city in the universe, Napier in New Zealand. Samantha's paintings are a masterful blend of form, style and content, incorporating the rich habitat she has encountered during her short itinerant life. Visit her facebook page Samantha Thompson—Artist or view her artwork at www.samanthathompson.com.au.

Pamela Utton—Page 13, 70

Residing in Baker, Florida Pam is a self-taught artist who has emerged her love of animals and art. In fact, it was her love of animals that inspired her to paint. Today, Utton is frequently called upon to paint pets from around the world. She is also an avid photographer and home designer. Her websites include pamutton.blogspot.com and her online store www.zazzle.com/pamutton. Visit her on facebook at "Pam Utton"

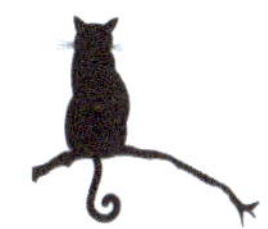

Chloe Wary—Page 72

Chloe is a cat, art and photography lover living in Paris France. See more of her work on facebook at Chloe Wary.

Tatjana Willms—Page 15, 39

Tatjana is a German self-taught artist. Her main style of art is the digital painting. She started to paint with pencil, watercolor, acrylic and more. Since 2007 she began to paint digital. She loves to draw fantasy portraits, mystic and Gothic themes. View her work at; www.tatjana-art.de, www.tatjanaart.com, www.zazzle.de/tatjanaart or on her facebook page "Mystic and Fantasy Digital Art of Tatjana Willms"

Valarie Wolf—Page 103

Valarie is an artist who resides in Orange County, California where she lives with her husband and two energetic Italian Greyhounds. Wolf is also a member of the American Academy of Equine Art. Valarie is passionate about animals in general and donates part of the proceeds of her paintings to various animal welfare groups. Learn more about Valarie and her art at www.valariewolf.com.

Kathryn Wronski—Page 54, 64

Painting dogs, cats, cows and pigs are among Kathryn's favorite subjects. Working from both customer's photos and her own, she creates and ships throughout the country. Kathryn does stray from time to time and paints local scenes of Northern California and Martha's Vineyard. View her work at; www.kwronski.com or contact her though her email at kwronski@sbcglobal.net.

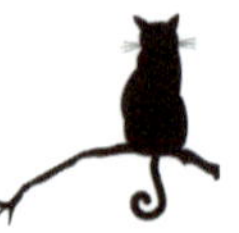

Index of Quotations

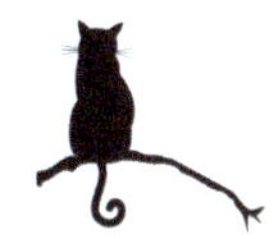

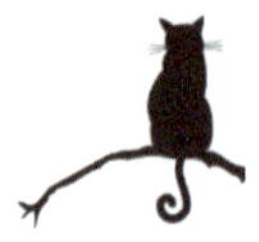

About the Author

BRADFORD G. WHELER is the former CEO, President and Co-owner of Allan Electric Company. He sold the company to a New York Stock Exchange listed company back when the stock market was hot. After staying on as President during the transition period, Brad retired.

Brad's lifelong love of history, art, books and the inherent humor in man's nature lead to the founding of BookCollaborative.com. and the publishing of this book as well as "HORSE SAYINGS: wit & wisdom straight from the horse's mouth", DOG SAYINGS: wit & wisdom from man's best friend", and "SNAPPY SAYINGS; wit & wisdom from the world's greatest minds".

Brad's various community involvements include being Chairman of the Board of Trustees of Cazenovia College, a member of the Board of Trustees of Community Memorial Hospital in Hamilton, NY, and Former Chairman & President as well a current member of the Board of Directors of Alumni Association of the Sigma Phi Society at Cornell University in Ithaca, NY. He is also a former member of the Board of Directors of the Greater Cazenovia Area Chamber of Commerce and several other boards.

Brad played polo on Cornell University's men's polo team for four years and was a member of the Cazenovia Polo Club. In 2012 he was inducted into the Manlius Pebble Hill Athletic Hall of Fame.

Brad holds a BS and ME in Civil and Environmental Engineering from Cornell University in Ithaca, NY as well as an MBA degree from Fordham University in New York, NY. He is a graduate of the Manlius Pebble Hill School. In addition he is a Licensed Professional Engineer.

Brad, his wife Julie, and their Golden Retriever Quincy live in Cazenovia, NY

www.ingramcontent.com/pod-product-compliance
Lightning Source LLC
LaVergne TN
LVHW052252100826
845147LV00001B/23

* 9 7 8 0 9 8 2 2 5 3 8 4 7 *